Gender and Democracy in Cuba

CONTEMPORARY CUBA

UNIVERSITY PRESS OF FLORIDA

Florida A&M University, Tallahassee
Florida Atlantic University, Boca Raton
Florida Gulf Coast University, Ft. Myers
Florida International University, Miami
Florida State University, Tallahassee
New College of Florida, Sarasota
University of Central Florida, Orlando
University of Florida, Gainesville
University of North Florida, Jacksonville
University of South Florida, Tampa
University of West Florida, Pensacola

Contemporary Cuba
Edited by John M. Kirk

Afro-Cuban Voices: On Race and Identity in Contemporary Cuba, by Pedro Pérez-Sarduy and Jean Stubbs (2000)

Cuba, the United States, and the Helms-Burton Doctrine: International Reactions, by Joaquín Roy (2000)

Cuba Today and Tomorrow: Reinventing Socialism, by Max Azicri (2000; first paperback edition, 2001)

Cuba's Foreign Relations in a Post-Soviet World, by H. Michael Erisman (2000; first paperback edition, 2002)

Cuba's Sugar Industry, by José Alvarez and Lázaro Peña Castellanos (2001)

Culture and the Cuban Revolution: Conversations in Havana, by John M. Kirk and Leonardo Padura Fuentes (2001)

Looking at Cuba: Essays on Culture and Civil Society, by Rafael Hernández, translated by Dick Cluster (2003)

Santería Healing: A Journey into the Afro-Cuban World of Divinities, Spirits, and Sorcery, by Johan Wedel (2004)

Cuba's Agricultural Sector, by José Alvarez (2004)

Cuban Socialism in a New Century: Adversity, Survival and Renewal, edited by Max Azicri and Elsie Deal (2004)

Cuba, the United States, and the Post–Cold War World: The International Dimensions of the Washington-Havana Relationship, edited by Morris Morley and Chris McGillion (2005)

Redefining Cuban Foreign Policy: The Impact of the "Special Period," edited by H. Michael Erisman and John M. Kirk (2006)

Ritual, Discourse, and Community in Cuban Santería: Speaking a Sacred World, by Kristina Wirtz (2007)

Gender and Democracy in Cuba, by Ilja A. Luciak (2007; first paperback edition, 2009)

Ritual, Discourse, and Community in Cuban Santería: Speaking a Sacred World, by Kristina Wirtz (2007)

The "New Man" in Cuba: Culture and Identity in the Revolution, by Ana Serra (2007)

U.S.-Cuban Cooperation Past, Present, and Future, by Melanie M. Ziegler (2007)

Protestants, Revolution, and the Cuba-U.S. Bond, by Theron Corse (2007)

The Changing Dynamic of Cuban Civil Society, edited by Alexander I. Gray and Antoni Kapcia (2008)

Cuba in the Shadow of Change: Daily Life in the Twilight of the Revolution, by Amelia Rosenberg Weinreb (2009)

Gender and Democracy in Cuba

Ilja A. Luciak

University Press of Florida
Gainesville/Tallahassee/Tampa/Boca Raton
Pensacola/Orlando/Miami/Jacksonville/Ft. Myers/Sarasota

14 13 12 11 10 09   6 5 4 3 2 1

First cloth printing, 2007
First paperback printing, 2009

Library of Congress Cataloging-in-Publication Data
Luciak, Ilja A.
Gender and democracy in Cuba / [Ilja A. Luciak].
p. cm.—(Contemporary Cuba)
Includes bibliographical references and index.
ISBN 978-0-8130-3063-0 (cloth: alk. paper)
ISBN 978-0-8130-3380-8 (ppk)
1. Women in politics—Cuba. 2. Women—Cuba—Social conditions.
3. Women—Government policy—Cuba. 4. Women's rights—Cuba.
5. Democracy—Cuba. 6. Cuba—Politics and government—1959–1990.
7. Cuba—Politics and government—1990– I. Title.
HQ1236.5.C9L83 2007
324.082'0972919–dc22   2007001293

The University Press of Florida is the scholarly publishing agency for the
State University System of Florida, comprising Florida A&M University,
Florida Atlantic University, Florida Gulf Coast University, Florida International
University, Florida State University, New College of Florida, University of
Central Florida, University of Florida, University of North Florida, University
of South Florida, and University of West Florida.

University Press of Florida
15 Northwest 15th Street
Gainesville, FL 32611-2079
www.upf.com

Für Carl David

Contents

List of Tables   ix

List of Abbreviations   xi

Preface   xiii

Acknowledgments   xxiii

Methodological Note   xxv

1. Gender Roles in the Revolutionary War: Initiating Change   1

2. Changing Gender Relations: The Social and Economic Sphere after 1959   13

3. The Cuban Political System: Competing Visions of Democracy   37

4. Party and State: Gender Equality in Political Decision-making   63

5. Gender Equality and Electoral Politics: The 2002–2003 National Elections   88

6. Conclusion: Gender Equality and Democratization   100

Appendix: List of Dissidents Sentenced in April 2003   113

Notes   117

Bibliography   129

Index   137

Tables

1.1. Gender Composition of FMLN Membership by Demobilization Category 10

1.2. Gender Composition of URNG by Demobilization Category, 1997 10

2.1. Women's Participation in the Structures of the Committees in Defense of the Revolution (CDRs), 1992–1998 30

2.2. Women's Participation in the Structures of the Cuban Workers Central (CTC), 1990–2000 30

2.3. Women's Participation in the Structures of the National Association of Small Farmers (ANAP), 1992–1999 30

2.4. Women's Participation in Leadership Positions, 1997 and 1999 33

2.5. Gender Composition of the Cuban Workforce and Percentage of Female and Male Leadership 33

2.6. Women's Participation in Leadership Positions, 2002 34

4.1. Women's Participation in Cuba's Poder Popular, 1976–2003 65

4.2. Gender Composition of Candidates to the Municipal Assemblies, 1976–2005 66

4.3. Gender Composition of the Municipal Assemblies, 1976–2005 67

4.4. Gender Composition of the Provincial Assemblies, 1976–2008 67

4.5. Gender Composition of the National Assembly, 1976–2008 68

4.6. Gender Composition of National Assembly Candidates Drawn from Municipal Assemblies by Province, 2003 77

4.7. Gender Composition of Cuba's Council of State, 1991–2003 79

4.8. Women's Participation in the Cuban Communist Party (PCC), 1993–1997 80

4.9. Gender Composition of the PCC's Leadership Structures, 1985–1997 81

4.10. Women's Participation in the Leadership Structures of the Communist Youth Movement (UJC), 1996–1999 85

5.1. Election Results to the Municipal Assemblies, 2002 93

5.2. Election Results to the National Assembly, 2003 95

5.3. Gender Composition of the Municipal Assemblies by Province, 2002 96

5.4. Gender Composition of the Provincial Assembly of Havana City, 2003 97

5.5. Gender Composition of the National Assembly by Province, 2003   98

5.6. Gender Composition of Cuba's Poder Popular, 2003   99

6.1. Gender Composition of the World's Parliaments, 2006   101

6.2. Gender Composition of the Revolutionary Left's Leadership Structures, 2001   102

Abbreviations

AMNLAE	Asociación de Mujeres Nicaragüenses, Luisa Amanda Espinoza (Association of Nicaraguan Women)
ANAP	Asociación Nacional de Agricultures Pequeños (National Association of Small Farmers)
CAI	Cooperativa Agropecuaria (Agricultural Cooperative)
CCS	Cooperativa de Crédito y Servicio (Credit and Service Cooperative)
CDR	Comité de Defensa de la Revolución (Neighborhood Committee)
CEA	Centro de Estudios sobre América (Center for the Study of America)
CEDAW	Convention on the Elimination of All Forms of Discrimination against Women
CNC	Comisión Nacional de Candidatura (National Candidate Commission)
CTC	Central de Trabajadores de Cuba (Cuban Confederation of Workers)
EU	European Union
FAR	Fuerzas Armadas Revolucionarias (Revolutionary Armed Forces)
FEDIM	Federación Internacional Democrática de Mujeres (International Democratic Federation of Women)
FEEM	Federación de Estudiantes de Enseñanza Media (Federation of High-School Students)
FEU	Federación de Estudiantes Universitarios (Federation of University Students)
FMC	Federación de Mujeres Cubanas (Cuban Women's Federation)
FMLN	Frente Farabundo Martí para la Liberación Nacional (Farabundo Martí National Liberation Front)
FSLN	Frente Sandinista de Liberación Nacional (Sandinista National Liberation Front)

INRA	Instituto Nacional de Reforma Agraria (Institute of Agrarian Reform)
IPU	Inter-Parliamentary Union
ONE	Oficina Nacional de Estadísticas (National Office of Statistics)
ONUSAL	Misión de Observadores de las Naciones Unidas en El Salvador (United Nations Observer Mission in El Salvador)
OPP	Órganos del Poder Popular (Organs of People's Power)
ORI	Organizaciones Revolucionarias Integradas (Integrated Revolutionary Organizations)
OSCE	Organization for Security and Cooperation in Europe
PCC	Partido Comunista de Cuba (Communist Party of Cuba)
SIDA	Swedish International Development Authority
UJC	Unión de Juventud Comunista (Union of Communist Youth)
UNDP	United Nations Development Program
UNEAC	Unión de Artistas y Escritores (Union of Writers and Artists)
UNICEF	United Nation's Children's Fund
UNIFEM	United Nations Fund for Women
UNRISD	United Nations Research Institute for Social Development
UPEC	Unión de Periodistas de Cuba (Union of Cuban Journalists)
URNG	Unidad Revolucionaria Nacional Guatemalteca (Guatemalan National Revolutionary Union)
USAID	U.S. Agency for International Development

Preface

Cuba has been mired in a serious economic crisis since the demise of the Soviet Union in 1991, when its key export market vanished together with billions of dollars in economic aid. Even before these cataclysmic events, the country suffered the impact of an economic embargo—a blockade, from the Cuban view—imposed by the United States more than four decades ago. Adding to these persistent problems was a substantial loss of revenues from reduced tourism in the wake of the September 2001 World Trade Center attacks. A rapidly changing world economy further complicated the economic picture. For example, plunging prices for sugar on the world market led to the drastic decision by the government to end raw sugar production for export, leaving the country without one of its traditional sources of income. As recently as the late 1980s, Cuba had occupied the position of the world's third largest sugar producer.

On the political front, Cuba is on the top list of countries the United States considers "terrorist states." President George W. Bush explicitly advocated regime change in speeches given in May 2002 and tightened the long-standing embargo even further following his 2004 reelection. In response to the threats emanating from the United States, the Cuban government initiated a crackdown on opposition groups. The April 2003 arrest of seventy-five Cuban dissidents, their subsequent harsh sentencing, and the execution of three hijackers of a ferry resulted in immediate, almost universal, criticism of the Cuban government. The European Union, which publicly condemned the actions taken by Cuban authorities, added its voice to those of established Cuban critics like the United States. Cuba entered a phase of considerable isolation while continuing to be a focus of the world's attention. With President Fidel Castro in ill health and having celebrated his eightieth birthday in August 2006, speculation surrounding the impending succession struggle was mounting, which contributed to the prevailing climate of uncertainty and insecurity. In short, Cuba was a country facing considerable challenges.

Every study that examines the Cuban political system is controversial from the outset due to the long-standing antagonistic relationship between the U.S. government and revolutionary Cuba. Cuba is under a U.S. economic embargo that has as its official justification the alleged dictatorial nature of the revolutionary government. The embargo itself is firmly opposed by the world community. In November 2006, for the fifteenth consecutive time since 1992, the United Nations General Assembly voted overwhelmingly in favor of a Cuban resolution to condemn the embargo. The vote on the nonbinding resolution was 183 to 4—the United States, Israel, Palau, and the Marshall Islands—while Micronesia abstained.

The U.S. government's criticism regarding the human rights situation on the island, however, is more likely to find open ears. Isolated in their economic aggression against Cuba, U.S. administrations find allies when they condemn the human rights record of the Cuban government. The European Union, while not acting in unison with the United States, has on several occasions severely curtailed diplomatic relations, most recently in 2003, and sought to apply pressure on the Castro government to open its political system.

Thus, an evaluation of the nature of Cuba's government always carries the implicit possibility of providing justification for U.S. policies, including the widely rejected embargo. On the other hand, a positive assessment of the revolutionary government's record is interpreted as support for a "dictatorial regime." Navigating between the Scylla and Charybdis of being considered an apologist for either side, the academic researcher has only one choice—to follow the path the research findings suggest. In the end, both Cuba and its critics can only benefit from studies that seek to contribute to a better understanding of Cuban reality.

Cuban officials are very sensitive to any outside evaluation that implies potential pressure to change the government in one way or another. Most importantly, Cubans demand to be treated as a sovereign nation and be judged only according to universally accepted norms. They justifiably oppose being singled out and held to a different standard. Ricardo Alarcón, president of the National Assembly, presented the official Cuban position on this subject when recently asked about Cuba's relations with the European Union:

> The relationship of the European Union with Cuba must be like the relationship Cuba has with any other country. We are not going to play with our sovereignty nor will we accept one condition, one requisite that would be different from the norms that determine the relations of Europe with the rest of the world. I think you know that the European Union has relations with all kinds of countries, with all types of societies. The intention and efforts to introduce conditions—this has been a reflection of the wish of North America. The United States asked this from Europe. It asked publicly, and some European countries, unfortunately, tend to comply with dictates from North America. And as is logical, if we have not given in to pressure from North America, in light of the blockade and before all the power of the United States, it would

be ridiculous to imagine that we would do so because of [pressure from] other states that are not as powerful.[1]

In this book, I avoid entering into polemics regarding Cuba's political system. Instead, I seek to contribute to a better understanding of the Cuban revolutionary process. I explore the following central research question: How does a revolutionary process affect women's role in society? I am interested in the relationship between revolutionary politics and substantive gender equality. I explore the thesis that the dynamics of revolutionary change can result in unintended consequences for women's emancipation. While socialist revolutions tend to be successful in fundamentally restructuring social and economic relations to benefit women, they have in general failed to bring about genuine equality in political decision-making. I maintain that Cuba's progress in guaranteeing women's social and economic rights and its success in guaranteeing women's formal political participation has ironically had *un-intended consequences:* it has inhibited a public debate on how to transform prevailing gender relations and preempted the emergence of an autonomous women's movement that could effectively advocate change. I concur with Julie Shayne's argument that the revolutionary government's effectiveness "in legally addressing women's basic needs . . . thwarted the want for a feminist social movement while allowing the government to claim that equality had been achieved."[2] This lack of mobilization, in turn, has been a key factor in explaining why Cuba has not made more progress on the path to substantive gender equality.

Whereas I provide an overview of women in the Cuban revolution, my focus is on the political sphere. In particular, I analyze women's role in political decision-making. In light of the argument that "one of the principal fault lines of democracy in the hemisphere is to be found in the exclusion of women from participation in the political systems of many countries,"[3] it is essential to assess women's role in Cuban politics. The Cuban revolution elevated equality in all areas of political, economic, and social life to be the main societal goal. From the very beginning, women's equality played a key role in the process of transforming society. Indeed, Fidel Castro considered women's emancipation to be "a revolution in the revolution."

A key argument of my study is that democracy cannot be successfully consolidated without the full incorporation of women into the political process both at the party and societal level.[4] Women's rights must be recognized, whether in their role as party militants or as citizens. Gender equality and meaningful democratization are inextricably linked. From a normative point of view, the democratization of the region requires the full incorporation of women as voters, candidates, and officeholders. Thus, the key analytical concepts that I rely on in exploring my central research question are *formal versus substantive democracy* and *formal versus substantive gender equality*.

Women political theorists have long recognized that "philosophical discussions of political democracy have been carried out largely in the absence of a discussion of women's rights or the impact of gender inequities on the function of a democratic political order."[5] In the Latin American context, Marysa Navarro and Susan Bourque argued in 1998 that "equal access to political participation and leadership remain distant goals for women in the region's newly constituted democracies," while acknowledging some positive trends for increased female participation during the last two decades.[6] The two authors criticize that "in the flurry of scholarly works on redemocratization in Latin America, and more specifically on the subject of democratic consolidation, relatively little attention has been paid to the question of women's participation."[7]

This trend is being reversed. Over the last decade, we have seen both an increased scholarly focus on women's role in decision-making and improved women's participation. The gender composition of decision-making structures in Latin America has become more equal, mainly due to the institutionalization of gender quotas. In the region, twelve countries adopted gender quotas since 1990. Argentina, Costa Rica, Ecuador, Mexico, and Panama can all point to great progress in changing the composition of their parliaments.[8] Cuba is not part of the "quota group," yet its Parliament is one of the most gender-balanced in the world. Notwithstanding this interesting statistic, Cuba remains a country that lacks an in-depth study on the gendered reality of political decision-making.

An extensive body of literature on democratization analyzes the "third wave" of democratization that started in the 1970s.[9] Whereas these studies initially focused on the breakdown of authoritarian regimes, they subsequently emphasized democratic consolidation. Some writers in this tradition tend to equate democracy with liberal constitutionalism. This normative focus leads analysts to emphasize the absence or existence of competitive party politics as the main indicator of democratic consolidation, instead of "the wider distribution of power in society [that] allows them to ignore gender inequalities."[10] A growing number of students of democratic transitions maintain that only a gendered analysis of democratization provides a meaningful picture of the social and political reality prevailing in a society in transition.

A number of excellent studies have been written on democratic consolidation in Latin America.[11] Most analysts agree that democracy cannot be reduced to the holding of elections. The overemphasis on formally competitive

elections as an indicator for the establishment of democratic rule is problematic because it severely limits our understanding of political and social
development. We need a more sophisticated analysis that entails a comprehensive concept of democracy. I concur with the growing number of scholars,
politicians, and practitioners who have warned of the dangers of seeking to
export and impose Western notions of democracy throughout the globe.[12] Afghanistan and Iraq are only the two most recent examples demonstrating the
complexities involved in "exporting democracy." Both countries held historic
elections in 2005, yet meaningful democratic rule remains elusive.

Larry Diamond is representative of those scholars who reject the restrictive
notions of the meaning of democracy. He understands it as encompassing "extensive protections for individual and group freedoms, inclusive pluralism in
civil society as well as party politics, civilian control over the military, institutions to hold officeholders accountable, and thus a strong rule of law secured
through an independent, impartial judiciary."[13] Similarly, Jorge Domínguez
and Mark Lindenberg understand the process of democratization as "the shift
to free, fair, and competitive elections, held at regular intervals, in the context
of guaranteed civil and political rights, responsible government (i.e., accountability of the executive, administrative, and coercive arms of government to
elected representatives), and political inclusion (i.e., universal suffrage and
nonproscription of parties)."[14]

According to these criteria, Cuba cannot be considered a democratic state.
The simple fact that Cuba is a one-party state and thus lacks "competitive elections" relegates Cuba to the realm of "nondemocratic" states. For example, in
the elections to the National Assembly, the number of candidates equals the
number of seats to be filled. I am not interested in engaging in polemics on
whether Cuba is a democracy or not. I argue simply that Cuba merits an in-
depth analysis on its own terms.

Cuban authorities tend to emphasize the substantive aspects of Cuban democracy and are proud to distinguish their political system from traditional
Western models. In general, the average Cuban does not view the electoral
process with the same interest as a European or U.S. citizen. For example, four
months before the first phase of the 2002–2003 election process that entailed
the selection of municipal assemblies was initiated, few Cubans had given the
process any thought. Many professed ignorance on whether elections would
be held at all. One former elected official emphasized, "Even the press has not
mentioned anything. . . . Until now [June 2002], I have not noticed whether
the elections were discussed. Yes, once we are in the election process, there
is radio and television propaganda, all the media always reminding people

that there will be elections."[15] The average citizen clearly understands that the electoral process does not have the significance it has in Western societies—in the end, elections do not affect the distribution of power.

Cuban reality can be elucidated through the key analytical concepts of formal versus substantive democracy and formal versus substantive gender equality. Gender is an analytical category that is helpful in demonstrating how socially constructed power relations affect women and men differently. This gender structure "contains an unequal power relationship with male domination and female subordination in most spheres of life."[16] Thus, gender needs to be understood as a socially produced category, defined in Terrell Carver's terms as "the ways that sex and sexuality become power relations in society."[17] Equality has two key dimensions, including formal equality, which is based on legal norms, and substantive equality, which presupposes a change in the power relations themselves.[18]

In the prevailing societal relations, both women and men are negatively affected. This view also leads to the conclusion that only men and women together can transform the inherited power relations. This conviction is at the core of the current emphasis on "mainstreaming" gender. Sustainable development and democracy require the explicit integration of a gender perspective: women and men must be in the mainstream of development. I argue that *sustainable development requires substantive democracy that is rooted in genuine gender equality.* The attainment of substantive gender equality, in turn, requires a transformation of societal consciousness.

Cuban officials point to the transformation of women's role in society as a key revolutionary achievement and act as advocates for women's rights in the international arena. For example, Cuba was the first country that signed the 1979 United Nations Convention on the Elimination of All Forms of Discrimination against Women (CEDAW), upstaging Sweden by one day. Notwithstanding Cuba's self-image on gender equality, Carollee Bengelsdorf's 1985 statement that "the Cuban experience with relation to women is problematic" is still valid.[19] She argued then that the Cuban situation "derives from inherited traditions and ways of doing things. A part of it is the legacy of underdevelopment and the unbroken constancy of external threat. But much of the problematic is demonstrated not simply by Cuba, but by all actually existing socialist countries, developed and underdeveloped."[20]

Again, it is a key argument of my study that gender equality policies pursued by revolutionary Marxist regimes such as Cuba can lead to *unintended consequences;* namely, an exaggerated sense of the country's achievements regarding substantive gender equality and the lack of an autonomous women's movement that could effectively argue for change in societal relations. I would like to emphasize the obvious point that gender equality remains a goal that no country can claim to have fully realized. Thus, we need to understand each country's record on its own terms and within a regional and international context.

I initiate my analysis with a brief discussion of women's contribution to the revolutionary struggle. Starting in the 1950s, women became actively engaged in support of activities to oust the regime of General Fulgencio Batista. Whereas the majority protested government policies by staging demonstrations in the cities, some women were involved in clandestine activities and supported the urban and rural armed movements that were active throughout the island. In this first chapter, I examine the gender-specific roles of women and men fighters. I then put the Cuban record in comparative context, relying on data from Central America.

In chapter 2, I analyze the changes taking place in the economic and social arena following the successful revolutionary war. I explore how women organized themselves to transform Cuban society after 1959, focusing on the role played by the Federation of Cuban Women (FMC). I examine the relationship of the FMC with party and government authorities and trace its development from a powerful grassroots movement into an organization that is considered by many out of touch with the challenges confronting today's Cuban women. I emphasize the enormous achievements women have made in health and education and discuss women's incorporation into the labor market. I argue that the Cuban government has succeeded in attending to practical gender interests but has made much less progress in transforming traditional gender relations. I seek to demonstrate that this is to a great extent due to the demobilizing effects of the Cuban approach to achieve gender equality, including the FMC's monopoly on women's organizing and its symbiotic relationship with the Communist party.

Chapter 3 examines the distinguishing characteristics of the Cuban political system and contrasts the Cuban view of democracy with established Western notions. I trace the evolution of the Cuban system of government, explore the question of pluralism, and assess the accommodating and oppositional traits of Cuban civil society. Whereas Cuba seeks to emphasize the substantive and participatory nature of its political system, foreign governments evaluate the Cuban revolutionary project from a traditional liberal constitutionalist perspective. This situation leads to unavoidable conflicts.

In chapter 4, I assess the progress Cuba has made over the past thirty years toward reaching the stated goal of establishing gender equality in decision-making. I explore the gender composition of Cuba's legislative structures, discuss efforts to strengthen women's political participation, and compare the inclusion of women into key state and party decision-making bodies. This chapter is guided by three main arguments. First, in Cuba's legislative structures, women have a greater presence at the national than at the local level, contrary to the experience of the United States and Western Europe. Second, despite the official position denying the existence of gender quotas, Cuba does implement measures of positive discrimination in order to strengthen women's presence in politics. I argue that Cuban reality requires corrective measures in order to improve gender equality in decision-making and that there is evidence that measures of positive discrimination, albeit not in the form of official quotas, are operative. Finally, Cuban women face a glass ceiling as they move up to positions of greater decision-making power, a reality familiar to women all over the world.

In chapter 5, I examine the role gender played in the 2002–2003 elections. These recent elections constituted an excellent opportunity to study the Cuban election process up close. This chapter complements the previous analysis by providing a detailed account of the nomination process and the gender composition of the decision-making structures at the local and national level that emerged from this contest. Although comprehensive studies have been published that examine Cuban elections, these studies lack a gender perspective.

I conclude with reflections on gender and democracy in Cuba and use data from Central America to put the Cuban experience in an appropriate comparative context. Cuba has established itself as a leader in guaranteeing women's basic economic and social rights. Few countries in the world provide better access to health care and education for their female population. Women's political participation is also respectable. Women do actively participate in the political process as voters, candidates, and officeholders. In some instances, particularly in the case of women's representation in the National Assembly, the Cuban record is excellent by international standards.

The favorable gender balance of Cuba's Parliament, however, is an apparent exception that confirms the following rule: I assert that an examination of the state of gender equality in Cuba's decision-making structures reveals an inverse relationship between the actual decision-making power of a particular institution and the presence of women. That is, the higher we get in the institutional decision-making hierarchy, the fewer women we find. Evidence for these arguments can be found by analyzing the gender composition of state and party structures.

Finally, the in-depth analysis presented in this book seeks to demonstrate that Cuba has succeeded more at the level of formal gender equality than in the substantive transformation of society toward equal political rights for women and men. The Cuban experience forces us to consider the consequences of policies that end up stifling the emergence of independent women's organizations and inhibit societal debate on the state of substantive gender equality. Whether the consequences are intended or unintended—as I argue in the Cuban case—the impact on societal development cannot be denied.

Acknowledgments

The research for this book was conducted with the financial assistance of the European Union. The views expressed are my own and in no way reflect the official opinion of the European Union. A special thank-you goes to Kristina Gardell, the first EU official to recognize the importance of studying gender in Cuba. Gardell was instrumental in the awarding of the EU grant. The successors in her position—Anne Caudron, Daniela Rofi, and Angelina Heerens—have also been very helpful.

I also acknowledge the substantial support provided by my home institution, Virginia Polytechnic Institute and State University. Xi Chen, my diligent research assistant, deserves particular praise, as does Kim Hedge, my executive assistant who formatted the manuscript. Furthermore, I am grateful to the Institute of Latin American Studies in Vienna, Austria, where I was affiliated during 2001–2002. The institute shared responsibility for the financial management of the project. Most importantly, I would not have been able to complete this research project without the generous assistance of many Cubans who shared their views with me. I am deeply appreciative of the confidence and the many signs of friendship that I have received. I am particularly indebted to Ricardo Alarcón and his office staff at the National Assembly. Ada Martínez, in particular, went beyond the call of duty to arrange interviews for me. I express my admiration for Sonia Moro, whose critical mind and love for the revolution embodies the best Cuba has to offer.

My wife, Jane, and my son, Carl David, share my love for Cuba. We traveled together on the island and experienced its remarkable people together. Our joint affection for the many inspirational accomplishments of the revolution has sustained me in the completion of this project. Seven years ago, at the age of eight, Carl David wrote an unprompted "letter to the editor" to the local newspaper. This published letter advocated the return of Elián González to Cuba to be with his father. I hope my son will see the day when North American and Cuban children can freely travel between their countries and learn from one another.

I am greatly indebted to the editors and anonymous reviewers of *Politics and Gender*, who were the first to provide comments on my Cuba materials. Their insights and constructive comments greatly strengthened my analysis. Similarly, Lorraine Bayard de Volo and Julie Shayne, who reviewed the manuscript for the University Press of Florida, deserve substantial credit for their excellent suggestions on improving the final draft. A final thank you goes to series editor John Kirk for his helpful comments.

Most of the material in chapter 4 originally appeared in "Party and State in Cuba: Gender Equality in Political Decision-making," *Politics and Gender* 1, no. 2 (2005). Several passages from chapter 2 and 3 were published in that same article. Several paragraphs from the preface, as well as from chapter 1 and 2, were previously published in *After the Revolution: Gender and Democracy in El Salvador, Nicaragua, and Guatemala* (Baltimore: Johns Hopkins University Press, 2001). The material is protected by copyright and is used here by permission from the publishers.

Methodological Note

Studying Cuba is unlike any experience I have had conducting research in Latin America over the past twenty-five years. Research in violence-torn Colombia or in Nicaragua, El Salvador, and Guatemala at the height of the revolutionary and counterrevolutionary wars seems easy in hindsight. Cuban authorities greatly restrict independent research on the island. Moreover, the complexities and idiosyncrasies of Cuban reality are difficult to capture and next to impossible to fully convey to the reader. By no means do I pretend to give a comprehensive view of gender and democracy in Cuba. Rather, I have chosen to focus on women's political participation.

This manuscript is based on field research conducted over a number of years. It is complemented by archival research and draws on election data and other official statistics. I have visited Cuba ten times, and my work is based on participant observation. For example, I had the privilege of observing the three days of voting for the June 2002 constitutional amendment and being invited to witness the constituent session of the municipal government of Havana Vieja in March 2003. On these occasions, I could see the Cuban model in action.

I interviewed forty key government officials, representatives of Cuban mass organizations, feminists, European Union ambassadors, and officials of the United Nations. In order to gain a perspective over time, several officials were interviewed more than once. I conducted structured interviews that were taped. In the manuscript, I am citing those officials that have gone on record by name. In some instances sources preferred to remain anonymous. In addition, I had numerous informal discussions with private citizens. Once one has gained their trust, people express themselves rather freely and can be quite explicit in their criticism of government policies. The writing for this book was informed by ten field visits to Cuba during February 1998, July 1999, October 1999, November 2000, February 2002, June 2002, November 2002, March 2003, April/May 2003, and November 2003.

Research about Cuba is always controversial. Most publications provide a one-sided, ideologically colored view of the island. In addition, very few studies are based on field research. The few works that do rely on primary data had to be authorized by the Cuban authorities and thus tend to present an overly sympathetic view of current reality. It is essential to be cognizant of the difficulties inherent in conducting research in Cuba in order to understand why so much that is being written about the island lacks any in-depth analysis.

My research had its own limitations. Under the best of circumstances, it is a Kafkaesque task to obtain a research permit from the Cuban authorities. During those times when the Cuban government perceives the international environment as particularly hostile—as it certainly did in the wake of the 2001 World Trade Center attacks while being on the United States' list of countries sponsoring terrorism—it becomes next to impossible. The U.S. government certainly does its part to raise suspicions for any researcher in the eyes of Cuban authorities. In a personal meeting, Ricardo Alarcón cited a letter from April 2002 in which the director of the United States Agency for International Development (USAID) "proposes to [U.S.] universities, to the academic institutions, to participate in a specific program in order to foment opposition groups in Cuba. It is much better to hide USAID. USAID is a government agency, but a university is something academic."[21] This letter, together with the official Track Two policy of the United States, which encourages the creation of civil society groups that oppose the Cuban government, provide ample justification for the Cuban authorities to make the life of independent researchers difficult. Suspicion is at such a level that it also affects researchers, such as myself, who are citizens of the European Union. If one adds to this the general reluctance of Cuban authorities to see independent research conducted that might result in criticism of any aspect of the Cuban revolution, it is easy to understand why research in Cuba is a challenging undertaking. This reality particularly affects any work that can be construed as potentially "subversive," such as my study on democracy and gender.

I never succeeded in finding a Cuban counterpart for my study, a requirement to obtain permission to officially conduct research in Cuba. I started the process in 1998 and, counting on the support of several high-ranking contacts I had developed over the years, appeared several times close to achieving it. The main problem was located in the Cuban Women's Federation (FMC), whose officials were extremely reluctant to approve independent research projects. All other Cuban institutions consider studies that focus on women to be the domain of the FMC and would refuse to get involved.

Due to these difficulties, a number of researchers have conducted "unauthorized" fieldwork on gender issues and other topics. In some instances, scholars have carried out research without being aware of the official policy regarding research permits or have chosen to ignore such requirements. Although these researchers have been able to talk with academics, independent feminists, and women from different walks of life, the lack of appropriate authorization curtailed their access to Cuban officials and limited the depth of their studies.

Fortunately, with the advice and help of close friends, I was able to establish contact with Ricardo Alarcón, president of the National Assembly. He offered help. On three separate occasions, his office facilitated and organized my contacts with Cuban officials. Without this invaluable assistance, I would not have had access to many of the high-ranking officials who granted interviews. It certainly helped that the European Commission funded my research, that I traveled with a European Union passport, and that EU officials endorsed my requests for work visas. Considering that Cuban-EU relations had entered a particularly rocky period at the end of my research, the cordial reception Cuban officials awarded me was remarkable. The cooperative, friendly atmosphere made it easy to bring up controversial subjects.

Members of the Cuban government or officials of the mass organizations give interviews only if they have a clear indication that these interviews are "authorized." Cuban citizens are understandably reluctant to talk to foreigners in any kind of formal setting, since they might be charged with violating laws that restrict the free exchange of information between Cuban citizens and foreigners. A number of journalists and researchers have been detained and/or arrested for violating their visa status when they established contact with opposition figures.

In order not to endanger my access to Cuban officials, I chose not to interview members of the various established opposition groups that exist on the island. Although such interviews would have enriched my analysis, they were not essential for my study. Despite my cautious approach, Cuban customs officials detained me in May 2003 while I was about to board my plane. Following a search of my hand luggage, the officials confiscated a document. The record in question was a listing of the seventy-five dissidents (with their sentences and their place of residence) that had been arrested and sentenced the month before.[22] This document had been originally faxed to numerous embassies and news organizations in Cuba and abroad by the Comisión Cubana de Derechos Humanos y Reconciliación Nacional, a dissident group headed by Elizardo Sánchez, an internationally known opposition figure.

Upon questioning, I informed the Cuban authorities that I had been given the document by a journalist who knew of my interest in gender issues and gave me the document as proof that there was only one woman among the seventy-five dissidents that had been sentenced. When I demanded to be given a justification for the confiscation of the document, I was told that the Cuban government did not recognize Sánchez's group and I was therefore in possession of an illegal document. Fortunately, I had permission to conduct research under my work visa and thus was not in violation of any immigration rules.

I have experienced difficult moments in my field research before. The Cuban incident certainly paled in comparison to a three-hour interrogation by Salvadoran immigration officials concerning the purpose of a 1988 field trip (four of my interview subjects were assassinated within months following my visit, including Segundo Montes, one of the murdered Jesuit priests), the fear I felt at the onset of the 6.3 Salvadoran earthquake of February 2001 while I was in the seventh-floor office of the country's parliamentary president setting up for an interview, or driving into an armed confrontation between Sandinistas and Contras on a mined road in northern Nicaragua in 1984. Nevertheless, it was an unpleasant experience.

It is not too difficult to understand the Cuban siege mentality. It is regrettable, however, that the lens most Cuban officials use to evaluate requests for research permits impedes them from distinguishing between the work of a bona fide researcher as opposed to the activities of an agent engaged in subversive actions on behalf of a foreign government. This has a chilling effect and, in the final analysis, it is Cuban society that suffers when independent analysis that can lead to constructive criticism is impeded.

Gender Roles in the Revolutionary War

Initiating Change

It is difficult to make a revolution without women's participation.
Orlando Lugo, president of the Small Farmers' Association

Historically, women's contributions to revolutionary movements have tended to be undervalued; they were generally not documented and thus easily forgotten. This changed in the 1980s and 1990s when women started to join guerrilla movements in massive numbers. Peace accords and the subsequent demobilization of guerrilla movements—those of Central America, for example—provided us for the first time with reliable data on the gender composition of these armed movements. This has led to the emergence of an increasingly important body of thought that examines women's participation in revolutionary movements. Karen Kampwirth (2002, 2004) and Julie Shayne (2004) are recent examples of authors exploring women's role in revolutionary struggle. In the case of Central America, I have argued that in order to understand and assess the role women play in the societies that emerged after successful revolution or in the wake of peace accords, we need to examine the contribution that women made during the phase of armed struggle.[1] The same argument applies to the Cuban revolution.

Women had actively participated in bringing about change in Cuban society long before the 1959 revolution. For example, *mambisa* (female independence fighters) fought side by side with their male comrades in the Cuban struggle for independence.[2] In the early decades of the last century, Cuban women were also on the forefront regionally in building a women's movement. In 1923 women from across the country got together and held a National Women's Congress. This was the first time in Latin America that women had been able to stage this kind of national event.[3] Their organizing translated into the progressive—for its time—1940 constitution that enshrined women's right to vote and to be elected to public office.[4]

In the 1950s women became actively engaged in support of activities to oust the Batista regime. In particular, high-school and university students were often in the vanguard. The majority protested government policies by engaging in open civil dissent, including staging demonstrations in the cities. Some women, however, got involved in clandestine activities and supported the urban and rural armed movements that were active throughout the island.

In this chapter, I explore women's contribution to the armed struggle. I first examine the gender-specific roles of female and male fighters. Subsequently, I put the Cuban record in comparative context, relying on data from the Central American revolutionary experiences.

Women's Gender-specific Contribution to the Cuban Guerrilla Movements

Timothy Wickham-Crowley, in his comprehensive study of Latin American guerrilla movements, found that female participation during the first wave of revolutions (1956–70) varied greatly. At the leadership level, exclusively male structures were not uncommon, although in some instances women represented up to 20 percent of the leadership. There were no cases of "female predominance in either numbers or power within a movement [and not] a single case of a female peasant joining as an arms-bearing guerrilla."[5]

It was the Cuban revolution that shaped the first revolutionary wave. Che Guevara, a key protagonist of the Cuban struggle, codified the lessons of guerrilla warfare learned in the Sierra Maestra in his book *Guerrilla Warfare*. His account became the bible for a generation of revolutionaries. Che recognized the importance of the potential contribution women could make to the revolutionary struggle. He emphasized that "the part that the woman can play in the development of a revolutionary process is of extraordinary importance."[6]

The women who supported the revolutionary forces joined a fight for social justice, not one for gender demands. Maria Teresa Peña, a combatant and subsequent cofounder of the Federation of Cuban Women, recounted recently: "I was not motivated by feminism. I only became conscious of women's problems after the [triumph of the] revolution."[7] In this regard, female Cuban revolutionaries did not differ from their Central American counterparts who fought a decade or two later. Only in exceptional cases did women from Nicaragua, El Salvador, or Guatemala have a gender consciousness when they decided to take up arms to fight repressive governments.[8] Thus, it is not surprising that female Cuban revolutionaries who grew up before the ascendancy of the international women's movement were not motivated by a desire to change prevailing gender relations.

Women, in general, were not particularly open to joining an armed struggle and thus assuming a countertraditional gender role. Karen Kampwirth has argued that the Catholic Church was the key institution in keeping the average

woman from daring to dissent. Examining the record of more recent revolutionary movements, Kampwirth finds that "no single factor distinguishes Nicaragua, El Salvador, and Chiapas from Cuba as clearly as liberation theology.
In Cuba, where the local Catholic Church promoted traditional gender roles,
either women were not mobilized in mass numbers or their mobilization was
not acknowledged by the revolutionary leaders."[9] Thus, the Cuba of the 1950s
was characterized by an absence of major challenges to prevailing gender relations. Nevertheless, Cuban women did join the revolutionary movement.
Knowledgeable sources estimate that about 300 women participated in the
guerrilla forces over time.

Similar to the experience of its Central American counterparts, the women
who rose to leadership positions in the Cuban movement tended to have a
privileged social background. Vilma Espín, one of the key women leaders of
the revolution, is a good example. Educated at the Massachusetts Institute of
Technology (MIT), her father was the vice-director of the Bacardi rum en-
terprise, while her mother was the daughter of the French consul in Havana.
Among the other female leaders of renown, Melba Hernández was a lawyer,
whereas Celia Sánchez and Haydée Santamaría came from middle-class families.[10]

Women played a variety of roles in the fight against the Batista dictatorship. They participated in the student movement organized into the Federation of University Students, were active in the 26th of July and the National
Revolutionary Movements, and held important positions on the Revolutionary Directorate.[11] A very select group of women occupied leadership positions
in the early days of the revolutionary war. In 1957 the urban leadership of
the National Directorate of the July 26th Movement included Celia Sánchez,
Vilma Espín, and Haydée Santamaría. At that point in time, Che himself had
yet to join the exclusive rank of the Directorate.[12]

The first female volunteer who is reported to have joined a guerrilla column
led by Che Guevara was Oniria Gutiérrez. She became part of the movement
in July 1957, at the age of seventeen.[13] It is reported that she argued with Che,
convincing him that if Celia Sánchez, the first woman to actively participate in
combat, could fight, so could she. At the time, women were only on occasion
permitted to take up arms.[14] The historic moment came in May 1957, when the
first woman actively engaged in combat against Batista's forces. It was "Celia
Sánchez, armed with an M-1 carbine."[15] A lifelong confidante of Fidel Castro, Sánchez became a figure of mythical proportions. During the war she
"took charge of communications and correspondence" and was considered
indispensable by Fidel Castro and Che Guevara.[16] Greatly admired, she chose
to remain in the background following the guerrilla victory. Yet behind the

scenes, Celia was known to work tirelessly to advance the revolution's interests. Cuban feminists point to her as a symbol for the "invisibility" of women's contribution to and their role in the revolution. They note that although her picture adorns the Cuban twenty-peso note, she can only be seen if one holds the note against the light, since Sánchez's picture is part of the watermark.

Che articulated the potential of women's contributions to armed struggle:

> The woman is capable of performing the most difficult tasks, of fighting beside the men; and despite current belief, she does not create conflicts of a sexual type in the troops. In the rigorous combatant life the woman is a companion who brings the qualities appropriate to her sex, but she can work the same as a man and she can fight; she is weaker, but no less resistant than he. She can perform every class of combat task that a man can at a given moment, and on certain occasions in the Cuban struggle she performed a relief role.[17]

In the Cuban context of the 1950s, when societal relations were characterized by *machismo*, this was an enlightened position. Interestingly, several important relationships between male and female revolutionary figures can indeed be traced to the days of the war. For example, Fidel Castro began a lifelong relationship with Celia Sánchez, while his brother Raúl met Vilma Espín, one of the original women fighters, whom he later married.

The Cuban women in the guerrilla movement clearly performed counter-traditional roles. This does not mean, however, that gender relations in the July 26th Movement were necessarily different from society at large. For example, men tended to resent women in command positions. Che recounts the reaction of some of his men that were under the command of a fighter named Lydia. He noted that she had led the camp "with spirit and a touch of high-handedness, causing a certain resentment among the Cuban men under her command, who were not accustomed to taking orders from a woman."[18]

Che reflected the traditional views of his time when he asserted that "naturally, the combatant women are a minority."[19] Indeed, few women served as armed combatants. While we have no official data on the gender composition of the Cuban guerrilla movement, most studies report that women represented about 5 percent of the combatants.[20] Women's combat readiness was highlighted with the 1958 creation of a platoon consisting exclusively of female fighters. The platoon took part in a number of important battles. It was named after Mariana Grajales, a Cuban independence fighter, and was led until the end of the armed struggle by officers Isabel Rielo and Teté Puebla.[21] The creation of this force is recognized as a pivotal event.

Nieves Alemañy, a high-ranking official of the Federation of Cuban Women, recounted the battalion's history and emphasized the role Fidel Castro played in its creation:

> [Fidel Castro] personally organized the battalion Mariana Grajales over the objections of his commanders. A group of men did not have weapons, and he armed the platoon of these women who until that moment had performed the work of nurses, teachers, making uniforms, doing "women's work." Women started to demand to participate in the war as soldiers. And even though there was a group of trained men without weapons, he gave the weapons to the women. Of course, the group of commanders and captains protested. But despite the protest, he created the platoon Mariana Grajales. He trained them himself.[22]

Although the platoon consisted of only fourteen women,[23] the symbolism was important. The fact that these women distinguished themselves in combat does not mean that they were exempt from tasks traditionally considered to be best left to women. Isabel Rielo herself affirmed that "even after becoming combatants, the Marianas [the members of the platoon] continued to perform more traditional tasks such as cooking and sewing in the rebel camps."[24]

Castro's support for female combatants shows an evolution in his thinking. Five years earlier, at the time of the attack on the Moncada barracks in Santiago de Cuba, Haydée Santamaría and Melba Hernández, the only two women that were part of Castro's fighting force of 165 people, were not allowed to "engage in combat, a restriction that infuriated Melba Hernández. . . . A compromise was struck; the women would go to Moncada, but as nurses to care for the wounded."[25] Their exclusion from combat was not a reflection of their leadership capacity. Indeed, after the failed attack on Moncada and the subsequent imprisonment of Castro and his associates, the movement was "managed largely by women: Melba, Haydée, Castro's sister Lidia, Natalia Revuelta, and to some extent his wife, Mirta."[26] Melba Hernández and Haydée Santamaría, who were also imprisoned in the wake of the Moncada attacks, received comparatively light prison sentences (seven months) compared to the male conspirators. The differential treatment of women and men fighters was one of the advantages women enjoyed in the revolutionary struggle that can be attributed to the prevailing gender relations. After Castro was released from prison in 1955 having served twenty-five months of his sentence, a select group of women continued to play a leadership role in the 26th of July Movement.

Guevara, the renowned guerrilla strategist, espoused traditional views, albeit with some important exceptions, on the distinct contribution women could make to the armed struggle based on their gender. In his vision, women were to serve mostly in support roles, such as teachers, social workers, and nurses attending to the guerrilla fighters and the population living in the zone of operation of the guerrilla forces. Che affirmed that the primary role of women was the following:

> Communications between different combatant forces, above all between those that are in enemy territory. The transport of objects, messages, or money, of small size and great importance, should be confided to women in whom the guerrilla army has absolute confidence; women can transport them using a thousand tricks; it is a fact that however brutal the repression, however thorough the searching, the woman receives a less harsh treatment than the man and can carry her message or other object of an important or confidential character to its destination.[27]

The "less harsh treatment" referred to by Che was potentially fatal, however. Jon Anderson, who has had access to Che's private diaries, gives an account of the tasks performed by Lidia, Che's "special messenger." Despite having three children,[28] she carried "the most compromising rebel communiqués and documents in and out of the Sierra Maestra to Havana and Santiago. These were highly dangerous assignments that involved crossing enemy lines, and would have meant her torture and almost certain death if she were caught. . . . Lydia was to become one of Che's most revered revolutionary personalities, a woman he exalted for exemplifying the virtues of self-sacrifice, loyalty, honesty, and bravery."[29] Another important female collaborator was Clodomira Acosta Ferrales. A former farmworker and maid recruited in June 1957, she "carried messages between various M-26–7 units in the Sierra, and later in the *llano*. Detained on a number of occasions, she always managed to talk her way to freedom. After each detention, Clodomira would mock the 'featherbrains' who released her."[30]

The history of Lidia and Clodomira, two revered figures of the revolutionary struggle, is important evidence that traditional gender relations indeed permitted women to be particularly effective collaborators. Nevertheless, they faced the same danger as the men. In the end, both women paid the ultimate price for their involvement in the struggle. While hiding in a safe house on a mission to the capital of Havana, they were captured by Batista security forces, tortured, and subsequently executed.[31]

Guevara appreciated the important role women could play in armed struggle, yet he was also a man of his time, espousing traditional gender views. This is evident when he argues for women to perform the "habitual tasks of peacetime. . . . The woman as cook can greatly improve the diet and, furthermore, it is easier to keep her in these domestic tasks; one of the problems in guerrilla bands is that all works of a civilian character are scorned by those who perform them; they are constantly trying to get out of these tasks in order to enter into forces that are actively in combat."[32]

Julie Shayne has developed the concept of women as "gendered revolutionary bridges" to capture these gender-specific roles outlined by Che. Shayne argues "that the contribution of women to both the popular and guerrilla movements were largely enabled and dictated by traditional notions of femininity."[33] Women tended to accept their subordinate role as part of the prevailing order. For example, Sonnia Moro, a member of the urban underground, helped with the creation of first-aid groups. Women's involvement with the struggle tended to be "invisible" in many regards. Shayne has argued that women's commitment in support of the revolution's goals, such as participation in a demonstration protesting government atrocities, was important in changing the perception the general public had of the guerrillas. It made the revolutionary movement less menacing and more accessible to the general public. Mothers and wives were naturally perceived as less threatening by the population and easier to identify with than armed guerrilla combatants. Therefore, women who were part of the popular movement opposing the authoritarian Batista regime were crucial in mobilizing support for the guerrilla forces and thus represented a bridge "between unincorporated civilians and the armed resistance."[34]

Most women who supported the revolutionary forces were not officially affiliated with them. Many were students who opposed the Batista regime and advocated change in the social and economic structures of the country. Mavis Álvarez, one of the cofounders of the Small Farmers' Association (ANAP), was typical of this kind of supporter. She was not directly affiliated with the revolutionary forces:

> I was a very young student. I was in the first year of my studies, and I participated in actions against the dictatorship, however, [it was] in people's actions: mobilizations, street protest, [and] confrontations with the police. And to the clandestine movement I gave support, but I was not old enough, nor was I formally integrated into a cell of the movement or had relations with the movement's leadership."[35]

Women's roles were a function of their gender. Sonnia Moro, who actively participated in the fight to oust Batista, recounted recently:

> Only now, a posteriori, do I realize to what degree I subordinated myself. How much they treated me as the little sister, how they impeded me from going to the most dangerous actions. . . . We worked in the infrastructure, secured safe houses, collected money and helped in mov-

ing things, checked out places for future actions, made plans, visited prisoners, [and] brought and took messages.[36]

Although most women remained in the background, they incurred the same risks as their male counterparts once their activities were discovered:

> In the beginning it was said that if they took a woman prisoner, apart from the fright nothing would happen to her. Afterward we found out about women being tortured and women being killed. We learned that the danger was the same [for men and women]. . . . At the moment of truth they would take you prisoner, they would torture you, and they would kill you because in the end you were against Batista. . . . It was an illusion to think that these actions were really minor ones because they were not, nor were they less dangerous. They thought that they were less dangerous, and this was the space that they gave to us. For them, direct action was dangerous, and not all of this connection business in which women played the major role. I had two defects. I was a woman and I was young. Those were two elements that limited me.[37]

Whereas women did participate in the Cuban revolution, few served as armed combatants, and most performed support roles. Contrary to the experience of the Central American guerrilla movements, women were not actively recruited. Karen Kampwirth has suggested four reasons why women were not sought after as combatants. Women's limited participation was a function of "the need for small numbers of guerrillas due to the foco strategy, the shortage of firearms, and the sexism of guerrilla leaders. . . . [In addition], in 1959, when Fidel's 26th of July Movement overthrew the Batista dictatorship, feminism played little role within international left-wing thought."[38]

Women's contribution to the revolutionary struggle tended to be less visible since it was concentrated in logistics. Here it is important to emphasize that the distinction between "combatants" and "women and men in support roles" is mostly artificial. In any army, the overwhelming majority of the personnel is engaged in logistics that support the front-line combatants. However, while their primary role is one of support, they are also "combatants." The war in Iraq has once again highlighted the danger facing those in supply missions. Furthermore, in the eyes of the guerrilla fighters themselves, the category of "combatant" was not limited to those bearing arms. Instead, as in any other army in the world, it included males and females in support roles. Thus, the exclusive focus on armed combatants tends to obscure and denigrate the important role played by women and men who provide logistical support.

The Central American Context

An examination of the gender composition of the Central American revolutionary movements helps us put women's contribution to the Cuban armed struggle into context. Women's participation in and support of the Cuban guerrilla forces did little to change the traditional gender relations prevailing in the culture of the revolutionary left. A decade later, when Central American women started to join guerrilla forces in El Salvador, Guatemala, and Nicaragua, they encountered the same stereotypes. Much had changed since the early days of the Cuban revolution, yet the basic challenges remained the same. It took fifteen years following the triumph of the Cuban revolution before women started to participate in greater numbers and armed women combatants were no longer viewed with suspicion. While we have scant accounts of women's experiences in the Cuban guerrilla forces, several important studies and testimonies provide insights into the life of women that served in the revolutionary movements of Central America and Mexico. The ascendancy of the international feminist movement accounts for this. It provided a context that was conducive to increased interest in the role of women in revolutionary struggles. Moreover, it opened the eyes of male guerrilla leaders to the potential recruiting pool women represented.[39]

The success of the 1979 Sandinista revolution in Nicaragua highlighted the significant role women had played in the insurrection. While it is clear that women participated in great numbers in the revolutionary struggle, the Sandinista National Liberation Front (Frente Sandinista de Liberación Nacional, or FSLN) never released official figures on the composition of its guerrilla force at the time of demobilization. For this reason, we are left with considerable variations in the reported estimates of female participation. It is commonly believed that at the high point of the Nicaraguan insurrection, women constituted between 25 and 30 percent of the combatants.[40] Women's participation in the Sandinista guerrilla movement increased over time. It can be analyzed in terms of three distinct phases. During the first phase, lasting from the origins of the FSLN in 1961 to the early 1970s, few women participated, and only in exceptional cases did they serve in combat roles. During this period, FSLN forces were extremely small, numbering only a few dozen fighters. Women joined in greater numbers during the second phase, which lasted from 1973 to 1977. This period marked a growing guerrilla movement, with women mainly in support roles. The last stage, 1977 to 1979, witnessed the massive incorporation of women into the armed struggle and coincided with popular uprisings in support of the FSLN.

Table 1.1. Gender Composition of FMLN Membership by Demobilization Category

Category	Women	%	Men	%	Total	%
Combatants	2,485	29.1	6,067	70.9	8,552	100.0
Wounded Noncombatants	549	22.2	1,925	77.8	2,474	100.0
Political Personnel	1,458	36.6	2,525	63.4	3,983	100.0
Total	4,492	29.9	10,517	70.1	15,009	100.0

Source: ONUSAL, *Proceso de desmovilización del personal del FMLN* (San Salvador: Imprenta El Estudiante, n.d.)

Table 1.2. Gender Composition of URNG by Demobilization Category, 1997

Category	Women	%	Men	%	Total	%
Combatants	410	14.8	2,368	85.2	2,778	100.0
Political Cadres	356	25.2	1,054	74.8	1,410	100.0
Total	766	18.3	3,422	81.7	4,188	100.0

Source: URNG, *Personal Incorporado*, pp. 2–4

In the case of El Salvador, we have excellent data due to the demobilization records compiled by ONUSAL, the United Nations Mission overseeing the disarmament process. Of the 8,552 combatants of the Farabundo Martí National Liberation Front (Frente Farabundo Martí para la Liberación Nacional, or FMLN) that were registered by the United Nations, 2,485 or 29.1 percent were female. In terms of the three demobilization categories, women were strongest among the political cadres, where they represented 36.6 percent. Overall, almost 30 percent of the FMLN membership was female.

The Guatemalan data, unfortunately, particularly in regard to the gender composition of the Guatemalan National Revolutionary Unity (Unidad Revolucionaria Nacional Guatemalteca, or URNG), are not as complete as those from El Salvador. This situation reflected the continued climate of fear within the country at the time of demobilization and the extremely secretive nature of the URNG. Nevertheless, a European Union–sponsored study of the socioeconomic background of the URNG membership gives a reasonably accurate picture of the URNG's gender composition. URNG members carried out this study during the demobilization process. The study is based on a survey of 2,778 URNG combatants (of the 2,940 concentrated in the demobilization camps) and 1,410 of the 2,813 political cadres. Although only half of the political cadres were surveyed, we have an almost complete picture of the URNG combatants.

According to table 1.2, women represented 410 (15 percent) of the 2,778 combatants and 356 (about 25 percent) of the 1,410 political cadres. These data demonstrate that compared to the involvement in El Salvador and Nicaragua, female participation in Guatemala's revolutionary struggle was rather limited. Among combatants (where we have the most complete data), the percentage of women in the URNG was only half as great as the number of armed female fighters in the Salvadoran guerrilla movement. Nevertheless, the data for all three Central American countries show that women's participation in armed struggle increased substantially since the Cuban revolution. The question to be raised—then as now—is to what degree women's participation in revolutionary armed struggle translated into increased political and social participation in the postwar period.

Conclusion

Women's participation as combatants in the Cuban revolutionary war was limited, yet they contributed in many areas to the success of the revolution. Contrary to El Salvador and Guatemala—where female combatants seeking to rejoin their families were frequently treated as outcasts by their own parents, siblings, and children for having abandoned their children during the war and were marginalized for having chosen the revolutionary struggle over their families—the Cuban women revolutionaries were welcomed with open arms. Cuba's situation was different from the reality of El Salvador and Guatemala, where peace settlements ended the wars without the guerrilla movements taking power.

As in Nicaragua twenty years later, once the revolutionary forces had taken power, its women were rightly considered part of the new vanguard and were admired. Yet there were certain similarities in the human suffering and upheaval caused by the war. In Central America, women combatants felt deeply humiliated when the armed struggle concluded and their comrades in arms, who had started relationships with younger women, abandoned them. This was also not uncommon in the case of Cuba. For example, one year before the revolutionaries took power, Che Guevara met Aleida March. Aleida had participated in the September 1957 uprising in Cienfuegos as well as in other armed actions. She had a reputation of being "extremely audacious, smuggling weapons and bombs around the province under her full-length fifties skirt."[41] Che fell in love with her. At the time he was married to Hilda Gadea, with whom he had a three-year-old daughter. Hilda had spent the war years in Peru, her native country. At the war's conclusion, she came to Cuba to find that her husband had taken a lover. Che ended up getting a divorce and married Aleida March.[42]

Having experienced the relative freedom and equality of combat, which was characterized by the predominance of nontraditional values, many women were reluctant to return to the straitjacket of gender inequality imposed by traditional societal norms. Thus they were eager to participate in the transformation of Cuban society that the revolutionary government advocated. Women played a key role in the social and economic reforms undertaken by the new regime.

Changing Gender Relations

The Social and Economic Sphere after 1959

[The] phenomenon of women's participation in the revolution was a revolution within a revolution. And if we are asked what the most revolutionary thing is that the revolution is doing, we would answer that it is precisely this—the revolution that is occurring among the women of our country!

Fidel Castro

Women's participation in the revolutionary struggle set the stage for a fundamental change in women's role in Cuban society following the January 1959 victory of the July 26th Movement, which ousted the dictatorship of Fulgencio Batista. Fidel Castro recognized women's participation in the struggle and eloquently advocated for the need to change prevailing gender relations. Cuban leaders today continue to highlight Castro's personal commitment to achieving gender equality. For example, Nieves Alemañy, a member of the National Directorate of the Federation of Cuban Women (Federación de Mujeres Cubanas, or FMC), affirmed: "When the revolution triumphed, in the first speeches, in the speech he gave in Santiago de Cuba before he arrived in Havana, he stated that one of the principles was [support for] women in the revolution.[1] From the beginning, the problem of women's equality is incorporated into the revolution's principles."[2]

Margaret Randall, one of the most astute and knowledgeable observers on the situation women confront in revolutionary societies, maintains that revolutionary movements have too often neglected to fight for women's rights upon assuming power. In her view, "socialism's failure to make room for a feminist agenda . . . is one of the reasons why socialism as a system could not survive."[3] Indeed, she considers the lack of a feminist agenda "a fundamental error of twentieth-century revolutions."[4] Richard Harris shares this position, emphasizing that "the historical evidence indicates that Marxism must be refocused to encompass the feminist perspective, and socialist regimes must take the appropriate steps to create the ideological context and material conditions for the genuine emancipation of women and the elimination of gender inequality in all its forms."[5] Cuba is one of the few remaining societies that continue to rely on Marxist principles. Its revolutionary government has had a long-standing public commitment toward gender equality. Thus, it is important to assess the Cuban record to establish what a revolutionary process that is approaching its fiftieth anniversary could accomplish.

Gender relations have changed dramatically since 1959. It has been well established that women have made great strides due to policies instituted by the revolutionary government. Initially, Cuban authorities sought to transform prevailing gender relations based on the premise that "the precondition of women's equality was the destruction of private property as the basis for state and family."[6] Following the reasoning of such Marxist thinkers as Friedrich Engels, the government would take on the responsibility of guaranteeing women's basic needs and establish equality in the public sphere through legislation.[7]

In this chapter, I analyze the changes taking place in the economic and social arena following the successful revolutionary war. I analyze how women organized themselves to transform Cuban society after 1959, focusing on the role played by the Federation of Cuban Women. I examine the relationship of the FMC with the party and government authorities and trace its development from a powerful grassroots movement into an organization that is considered by many out of touch with the challenges confronting today's Cuban women. I emphasize the enormous achievements women have made in health and education and discuss women's incorporation into the labor market. I argue that the Cuban government has succeeded in attending to practical gender interests but has made much less progress in transforming traditional gender relations. I seek to demonstrate that this is to a great extent due to the demobilizing effects of the Cuban approach to achieve gender equality, including the FMC's monopoly on women's organizing and the organization's dependence on the Communist party.

The Creation of the Federation of Cuban Women

Women were organized throughout the country following the revolution's victory. The key organizational force facilitating women's participation was the Federation of Cuban Women, founded on August 23, 1960. The Federation had its roots in a variety of women's organizations that emerged in the early twentieth century. They included the Comité de Sufragio Feminino (Women's Suffrage Committee, founded in 1912), the Club Feminino de Cuba (Women's Club of Cuba, 1917), the Federación Nacional de Asociaciones Femeninas (National Federation of Women's Associations, 1917), and the Unión Nacional de Mujeres (National Union of Women, 1934). These groups, in coalition with several others, were effective in getting women the right to vote in 1934. A few years later, in 1940, progressive labor and maternity legislation was introduced. Indeed, in terms of women's rights, Cuba had "one of the most progressive constitutions in the hemisphere" even before the revolution.[8]

When Castro's forces took power, more than 920 women's organizations existed in the country.[9] Within a short time these groups were subsumed into the FMC, leading to explosive growth in its membership. Two years after it was founded, the FMC had more than 400,000 members. A decade later, the FMC had grown to 1.9 million. At the time of its fifth Congress in 1990, 3.2 million women had joined the organization.[10] In 2000 the FMC comprised a membership of more than 80 percent of Cuban women over the age of fourteen. However, since almost every woman is a member of the organization, the meaning of membership has been greatly reduced. The organization has established a presence throughout the country with 78,000 structures at the neighborhood, municipal, provincial, and national level. At the local level, it functioned as a voluntary organization. Paid professionals existed only from the municipal level up.

The FMC effectively served as a transmission belt for the party. At the height of its prestige in the late 1970s and early 1980s, the FMC was considered the most important grassroots organization. It was an important voice for Cuban women and the key organizational force behind the many positive changes in the daily lives of Cuban women.

Attending Practical Gender Interests: Health Care and Education for Women

Maxine Molyneux has argued that the difficulty every revolutionary regime faces in devising the best strategy for achieving gender equality has its roots in the difficulty of defining women's interests or explaining the roots of women's subordination. She maintains that "women's oppression is recognized as being multicausal in origin and mediated through a variety of different structures, mechanisms, and levels, which may vary considerably across space and time. There is therefore continuing debate over the appropriate site of feminist struggle and over whether it is more important to focus attempts at change on objective or subjective elements, on structure or men, on laws and institutions or on interpersonal power relations—or on all of them simultaneously."[11] Molyneux makes an important distinction between strategic and practical gender interests that elucidate the Cuban context:[12]

> Strategic interests are derived in the first instance deductively, i.e., from the analysis of women's subordination and from the formulation of an alternative, more satisfactory set of arrangements to those that exist.

These ethical and theoretical criteria assist in the formulation of strategic objectives to overcome women's subordination, such as the abolition of the sexual division of labor, the alleviation of the burden of domestic labor and childcare, the removal of institutionalized forms of discrimination, the establishment of political equality, freedom of choice over childbearing, and the adoption of adequate measures against male violence and control over women. . . . Practical gender interests are given inductively and arise from the concrete conditions of women's positioning by virtue of their gender in the division of labor. In contrast to strategic gender interests, practical gender interests are formulated by the women themselves who are within these positions rather than through external interventions. Practical interests are usually a response to an immediate perceived need, and they do not generally entail a strategic goal such as women's emancipation or gender equality.[13]

In addition to the difficulty of designing an effective strategy to strengthen gender equality, the new government faced the same dilemma that confronted the Sandinista leadership of revolutionary Nicaragua, which took power two decades after its Cuban counterpart; namely, whether to give priority to the overall goals of the revolutionary project or to satisfy specific sectoral interests, in this case those of women. Similar to the Sandinistas, the male-dominated Cuban leadership defined what constituted "the interest of the revolution" and proceeded to implement its policies toward women based on the premise that all group interests had to be subordinated to the revolution's survival.[14]

The early focus of the revolutionary authorities was on practical gender interests, including changing women's access to health care and education. It is widely recognized that the changes instituted by the revolutionary government led to "above-average levels of progress for the Latin American region on key indicators such as female mortality, educational levels, legal rights, healthcare and employment."[15] Women benefited as part of the population targeted by the various revolutionary initiatives to improve the life of the Cuban people. For example, the 1961 literacy campaign brought one hundred thousand volunteers into the countryside, where they experienced the living conditions of the peasantry first hand. More than half of these volunteers were "young girls, many of whom went in active defiance of middle-class parents who had rigid and traditional ideas about the proper realm for their daughters' activities."[16] Naturally, traditional gender relations were affected by these experiences.

Women's participation in the Cuban revolution translated into greater societal participation following the 1959 victory. This was particularly the case for rural women. Mavis Álvarez, a leader of the Asociación de Agricultores

Pequeños (Association of Small Farmers, or ANAP), recounted how female peasants got involved in building a new society:

> When the revolution triumphed, peasant women had principally a domestic role. Very few women in the countryside participated in an important community activity, much less did they have influence in the community. Those [who did] were exceptions. The revolutionary struggle permitted women to distinguish themselves as a force on which one could count, a useful force. As in almost all wars, it is in war that the woman takes on the role as guardian of the family and the community and assumes precisely a very important leading role.
>
> Yet when the revolution triumphs, [it becomes clear that] the woman who has actively participated in the revolution is the [same] woman that had already held a social leadership role. But they are not many. Still, the great mass of peasant women, the great majority of peasant women, have not had the audacity to take part socially, and it is the revolutionary activity itself that offers her possibilities of participation, including in the literacy campaign, the health campaigns, the constitution of the peasant organizations themselves. Thus, women were not excluded. On the contrary, women were actively recruited into these organizations, and this was the work of ANAP. [It was] an important effort by ANAP to give the peasant woman a participatory space also.[17]

Strategic versus Practical Gender Interests

In its early years, the FMC served mainly as a mobilizing vehicle to rally women in support of the goals set by the revolutionary leadership. Vilma Espín, the FMC's founding director and a renowned revolutionary leader in her own right, acknowledged that the initial objectives pursued by the organization "were not oriented to gain partial revindications for women alone, but to unify them, and to mobilize them, so we could constitute a powerful force that could defend, support and fight for the revolution."[18] Women benefited as a part of the previously marginalized majority of the population. For example, the FMC played a central role in the literacy campaign, which empowered thousands of women. Yet the fact that women gained access to education, health care, and land, and were integrated into the workforce, made them less likely to fight to change traditional gender relations. Julie Shayne has argued that the "establishment of women-focused social services almost immediately following the revolutionary triumph preemptively thwarted the want for a feminist social movement while allowing the government to claim that equality had been achieved."[19] According to her analysis, satisfying women's practical needs decreased the likelihood of feminist mobilization.

The initial focus on practical gender interests changed once the FMC and other organizations realized that traditional gender relations needed to be attacked more directly for change to occur.

> There came a moment when Cuban society itself and the Federation of Cuban Women, which had accumulated considerable experience in this, observed with concern that women's progress is not as rapid and as profound as the revolutionary laws themselves promoted. . . . No one changes what suits him, what agrees with him, what works for him. No one changes without resistance. And for men, the type of [traditional gender] relations in the countryside worked very well—the type of relationship in which the man has the dominant voice. Where the man [and the woman] work, but when the woman arrives home she is his servant and the servant of the family.[20]

Based on this insight, the 1970s saw a more proactive approach by the FMC in its advocacy for gender equality. One reason for the call to action was the difficulty women faced in increasing their participation in political decision-making. Viewed through a gender lens, Cuba's initial exercise in electoral democracy—the 1974 trial election in Matanzas Province—was problematic. Only 7.6 percent of the candidates were female, and of the elected delegates a mere 3 percent were women.[21] Fidel Castro criticized this outcome and called for an investigation to find the underlying reasons.[22] Not surprisingly, an FMC study found that women were unable or reluctant to assume any political commitments on top of their normal workday and in addition to the many hours they spent to attend to the needs of the household. To alleviate women's workload, it was proposed that "housework [be] shared among all family members—female and male, adults and children."[23] This proposed solution became part of the Family Code.

The 1975 approval of the Código de Familia (Family Code) was a key FMC achievement. The code was the culmination of an effort to change women's role in society through a series of legal measures. There is no question that the Cuban government instituted a series of laws that were very progressive in nature, whether they concerned women's equality, labor standards, or reproductive health.

The new code mandated changes in the private sphere of the household toward a relationship built on gender equality. Articles 27 and 28 were particularly controversial:

The partners must help meet the needs of the family they have created with their marriage, each according to his or her ability and financial status. However, if one of them only contributes by working at home and caring for the children, the other partner must contribute to this support alone, without prejudice to his duty of cooperating to the above-mentioned work and care.

Both partners have the right to practice their profession or skill and they have the duty of helping each other and cooperating in order to make this possible and to study or improve their knowledge. However, they must always see to it that home life is organized in such a way that these activities are coordinated with their fulfillment of the obligations posed by this code.[24]

Although violation of these articles could be grounds for divorce, these provisions were generally not enforced.[25] The code was effective in the sense that it established societal goals and served as a point of reference. No one expected gender relations to change overnight, and change was slow in the countryside in particular. The code "drew attention to a problem. Because if you must promulgate a code, it is because a problem exists. There is a societal problem that the code seeks to address."[26] The code was significant because it sought to change gender relations at the core of society—within the family itself. Women leaders who advocated change recognized this truth: "It is in the heart of the family where gender relations are most practiced, and this determines the formation of man and woman and the attitudes [they hold] later on in society."[27]

The progressive nature of the Family Code should not prevent us from recognizing that its promulgation became part of the *unintended consequences* such policies had. For example, Shayne has argued that the Family Code actually inhibited change since "there was even a backlash against women's rights as Cuban society perceived itself to be more evolved than other nations with respect to gender relations."[28] Indeed, at the same time that Cuba had established one of the most progressive legal frameworks in support of women's equality, FMC officials were reluctant to embrace the agenda of the international feminist movement. Feminism was rejected because it was perceived as representing Western notions of women's emancipation that were potentially in conflict with the Cuban model. This included an initial rejection of the usefulness of gender analysis.

The Controversy over Feminism and Gender

Until recently, Cuba differed from other Latin American societies in having been isolated from international trends. Whereas the international movement in favor of gender equality that gathered strength in the 1970s and became a force in the 1980s influenced developments in the region, this was not the case in Cuba. The primary international contacts were with women's organizations from the socialist bloc and other leftist movements organized in the International Democratic Federation of Women (Federación Internacional Democrática de Mujeres, or FEDIM). By the 1980s, however, Cuba started to be exposed to the international gender equality agenda. Mavis Álvarez, in charge of the international relations department of ANAP, the Small Farmers Movement, affirmed:

> We had dark years. Remember that Cuba was expelled from the OAS (Organization of American States). Cuba practically didn't exist for the world. There were some years—between 1959 and 1970—when our relations where fundamentally with the socialist countries. The role women played in the socialist countries were an example for us. Because women had made a lot of progress in these societies. . . . Wherever you looked we saw women actively participating. This was the example that motivated Cuban women and Cuban organizations a lot. But outside of this context, Cuba had few relations with the [rest of the] world. We were ostracized. And to the extent that Cuba started to move in the world, to participate in international events . . . agencies of the United Nations, such as UNICEF, started to work actively in Cuba, and in their campaigns and in their work, women played a very active role. This started to influence the thinking of the Cuban authorities and women themselves, particularly the women's organization, the Federation of Cuban Women. And the party itself started to give more room to a greater number of women and began to realize that the party as the leading force in society needed to speak up. . . . At this point, the party started to demand that the mass organizations define a strategy and pronounce themselves politically in their work for greater women's participation.[29]

Thus, the international discussion on gender and its implications for societal relations had a delayed impact in Cuba. With increased international contacts, however, the gender perspective gained prominence, and with it came a reexamination of women's role in society.

Within the region, officials from the Women's Federation were exposed to feminist organizing and thought at the various Latin American "encuentros."

Starting with the 1987 meeting in Taxco, Mexico, feminists and representatives of women's groups from Latin America and the Caribbean got together to discuss the state of women's organizing and develop an agenda for action. Feminists from Nicaragua and El Salvador, who came out of the revolutionary movements of their countries, were particularly active in the early years of these meetings.[30] FMC officials learned from their sisters who shared a similar experience of revolutionary struggle and subsequent building of a women's movement. For over a decade, FMC representatives were the only Cuban participants at these meetings. Cuban feminists have emphasized that the FMC delegates did not actively share these regional discussions once they had returned home. Non-FMC women activists were able to break the organization's attendance and information monopoly in 1999, when they started to participate in these meetings.[31]

In the 1990s the Women's Federation endured increasing criticism. Although the FMC was active in pointing out some of the challenges confronting women, it exhibited considerable limitations. Knowledgeable observers maintained that the FMC was "out of touch with the problems of Cuban women today."[32] Most importantly, the federation's leadership was criticized for being reluctant to incorporate gender analysis into its work and seeking to suppress any efforts by women to organize outside the official organization. The FMC's problems were also attributed to socialist ideology, which equated women's economic freedom with their liberation.

> Socialism liberated women by putting them to work. Just like that. If you were salaried, you were liberated; if you worked productively, you had already broken your chains. In the socialism that we learned, everything was so easy, everything went in a straight line: society emancipated itself from capitalism and everyone was happy; everything was now functioning. Women emancipated themselves economically and were now free. The family subordinated women; work liberated women. What sheer foolishness, gentlemen![33]

The organization's resistance to engage in a critical reevaluation of the state of gender relations some thirty years into the revolutionary process, manifest in its refusal to adopt "gender" as an analytical category, became a rallying cry for a small group of women who recognized the contributions gender analysis could make in addressing the continuing inequality between women and men.[34] In their view, gender analysis was useful in demonstrating how socially constructed power relations that had emerged in post-1959 Cuba affected women and men differently.

As it has been described in the case of other societies, the prevailing gender structure "contain[ed] an unequal power relationship with male domination and female subordination in most spheres of life."[35] Since men were privileged in these hierarchies of power, they could be expected to resist change. It was therefore important to bring men into the dialogue on gender equality.

A Cuban feminist, at the forefront of these developments, recounted the introduction of the gender concept into the discourse of the time: "The gender problematic was studied by us in Magín [an independent women's group].[36] Later, the federation also used this concept. However, in my opinion, it remained in the scientific events, in the meetings . . . but here at the grassroots level it did not exist. It would be interesting if all women knew what gender is."[37]

The gender concept was introduced to Cuba via Mexico. One of the island's early proponents of gender analysis recounted this process:

> It came here in the year 1990 with a group of Mexicans who organized a women's forum at the Casa de las Américas [a publishing house]. And starting from there, they invited a group to come to Mexico in 1991, and this began this whole machinery. The federation entered later. Really, they joined because they had no other choice. And I see it as a concept artificially incorporated. . . . Still there is a resistance. Last year [2002] the vice president of the federation said: "It doesn't make sense to speak of feminism. This has no relevance for the federation."[38]

Indeed, contrary to the views embraced by many women's organizations throughout Latin America, the FMC had a pronounced "non-feminist" position. It considered itself, in the words of Vilma Espín, "feminine, not feminist."[39] In official Cuba, feminism tends to be viewed as "extreme" and thus divisive. In Julie Shayne's view, this reality "stem[s] from the pejorative meaning the Communist Party has superimposed upon the idea of feminism, and thus feminists. That is, Cubans have repeatedly heard that feminism is a divisive, Western, bourgeoisie [*sic*], imperialist concept that encourages man-hating."[40] It is this presumed divisive quality of feminism that is threatening to Cuban officials, since any idea that potentially divides society endangers the revolutionary project.

On this issue, there appears to be a split within the FMC, with some officials embracing the gender concept and feminism publicly, whereas others espouse more traditional views. Concepción Campa, one of only two women on the party's Politburo and a member of the FMC's National Directorate, represented the view of those that were concerned about the divisive nature of "feminism":

The federation does not function at any moment based on a concept of extreme feminism. Neither extreme nor not extreme, it does not function as a feminist movement that divides the genders. Otherwise, we would be doing the opposite of what we should do. The federation functions based on the search for equilibrium between the feminine and the masculine. It does not follow the tendency to divide men and women but to unite them in a struggle or a common cause, which involves the nation's social and spiritual development at all levels.[41]

Whereas federation officials expressed reservations concerning feminism, they were more accepting regarding the usefulness of gender analysis. Several key FMC leaders, including Nieves Alemañy, the official in charge of the Department of Organization, insisted that the federation's activities do have a gender focus. For example, Alemañy emphasized that the organization's work at the grassroots level "is directed toward women but also toward men. Some of the people who are attended to are men."[42] Those in favor of gender analysis point out that Fidel Castro himself has consistently used a gender lens to view relations between the sexes in Cuba. In Alemañy's eyes, "From the first years of the Revolution he had it incorporated into his analysis, even though it still had not been identified as a category of analysis."[43] Apart from their individual positions on feminism and gender analysis, all FMC leaders agree that gender equality is a societal goal. According to Politburo member Campa, strengthening gender equality "is the wish of Fidel himself." In her view, "It would be difficult to find a head of state that respected women quite as much as Comandante Fidel."[44]

In the months leading up to its 1990 congress, the FMC decided to focus its agenda for the coming years on women's political participation and their role within the family structure. The campaign "cut into politics at every level, from the obstacles to women's advancement in the formal political structure to a reaffirmation of women's politics, family politics, and the politics of sexuality."[45] The FMC's new emphasis came at a time when the organization had to reinforce its relevance in the eyes of its core constituency. A survey conducted a week before the congress "revealed widespread indifference to the FMC," with two-thirds of the respondents professing ignorance that the FMC was about to convene a national meeting.[46] The leadership had to face the challenge that the organization had lost its relevance, while continuing to serve as the national advocate for women's rights.[47] There was disagreement among women activists on whether FMC chapters at the local level continued to make a difference, while there was a consensus that the national leadership was acting in a vacuum.

The attempt by the organization to refocus its work never bore fruit. The reform agenda had barely been formulated when it was abandoned due to the severe economic and political crisis engulfing Cuba in the wake of the Soviet Union's demise. The economic crisis of the 1990s created severe problems. According to the FMC, between 1990 and 1994, female employment in the state sector was reduced by 31.5 percent.[48] Instead of a reform agenda, "defense" of past achievements, including health-care and education policies benefiting women, carried the day.[49] The revolution's achievements indeed needed defending during the 1990s. For example, the economic crisis had seriously eroded the state's capacity to deliver basic health care. There was a shortage of basic medicine and supplies. The deteriorating conditions forced women giving birth to bring their own sheets for their hospital stay. Yet Cuban doctors continued to offer their considerable expertise free of charge, and by all accounts, scarce resources were allocated equitably. Like many times before, the Cuban people endured.

Thus, the FMC leadership did not want to push an agenda that could be divisive at a time when the country was close to economic collapse and Cuban exiles based in Florida were already discussing what policies to implement following their return to power. This decision effectively locked the FMC into a time warp and played a key role in the organization being increasingly considered to be out of touch with the reality experienced by Cuban women. The FMC was caught in its eternal dilemma to reconcile the organization's "dual function as a promoter of women's equality and arm of the party."[50]

Autonomy from the Party

Cuban law establishes the FMC as a nongovernmental organization (NGO). Yet the FMC cannot be considered an NGO since the organization lacks the autonomy that is essential to be considered truly "nongovernmental." Margaret Randall put it succinctly: "[The FMC] was and is controlled by the Cuban Communist party."[51] Vilma Espín, the FMC's historic leader, affirmed this reality, recounting that "it was Castro himself who asked her to form the FMC in an effort to strengthen the revolution in light of the counterrevolutionary threat."[52] Indeed, party policy is generally indistinguishable from FMC policy.

The FMC used to be financially dependent on state support. According to FMC officials, the federation is now supporting itself from its own resources. Individual membership contributions represented the bulk of the FMC budget of twelve million Cuban pesos.[53] In addition to the ten million collected in dues, the organization had about one million pesos in income from its publications and another million from a variety of instructional seminars offered by FMC personnel.[54] Yet this apparent financial independence did not translate into anything approaching autonomy. The shift to self-supporting finances was a reflection of the decreased capacity of the Cuban state to provide financial support and was not accompanied by a redirection of the FMC leadership toward greater institutional independence from the party.

The federation is an extremely hierarchical institution, and its structures are modeled to parallel those of the party. It is this symbiotic relationship with the party that has limited the organization's development. For example, it has been argued that "because most initiatives for 'sexual equality' in revolutionary Cuba came not from women themselves but from male elites, women through the years showed more interest in obtaining state assistance to ease family duties than in increasing female representation in power."[55] The FMC leadership views its main mandate as generating support for the revolutionary project. This leads the federation to defend the current state of affairs instead of advocating change, turning it into an impediment to progress toward greater gender equality.

This was evident in the early 1990s, when the federation's conservative leadership resisted calls by feminists to openly adopt gender analysis as a useful lens to examine the challenges confronting Cuban women or when it sought to suppress any efforts of women's organizing outside the organization. A case in point was the "deactivation" of Magín, the Association of Women Communication Workers.

Deactivating and Preempting Independent Women's Groups: The Case of Magín

Criticism of the FMC came from a plethora of sources in the mid-1990s. In the eyes of a number of important female leaders who are sympathetic to the revolution, "the women's organization does not exist at the grassroots level. . . . Some thought that the Federation of Women didn't make sense any more. There was a discussion whether the current structure of the federation should continue to exist. They saved it, but it exists only on the top, it does not remain below."[56] Another activist concurred: "I knew the work [of the FMC] at the block level. The work of the federation was visible. We got the people together and had a monthly debate on health care. There were a lot more activities of a collective nature. . . . However, in my opinion, at this point, I don't see the work of the federation at the grassroots level. We are never called to a meeting."[57]

Some questioned whether the federation could adapt and effectively represent women's interests at the turn of the millennium. "The problems women experienced on January 1, 1959, in Cuba are not the same the woman of today confronts. . . . The problems of violence [against women] exist, maybe not as they might exist in Mexico. Well, we are in Havana, but they exist. The problems of prostitution in Cuba exist. Maybe not as in the capitalist societies, but they exist. Thus the work is unfinished. We must keep it up, [regardless of] the many achievements we might have."[58] Feminists, in particular, felt increasingly alienated from the FMC. Some argued that it was time to create new initiatives to advance gender equality.

One concrete outcome of these deliberations was the 1993 creation of the Association of Women Communications Workers (Asociación de Mujeres Communicadoras, or Magín). The inspiration behind the creation of Magín was the First Iberoamerican Women and Communication Congress that was held in Havana. At this meeting, several future Magiñeras were introduced to the "gender" concept.[59] Julie Shayne has argued that Magín represented "an organization of utmost importance in tracing the evolution of a feminist consciousness in Cuba."[60] The main objective of the new collective was to change women's image in the media. The women involved represented diverse sectors of Cuban society, including journalists, historians, and artists. The founding members were all affiliated with the FMC. Initially, federation officials participated in some of Magín's meetings, and relations remained cordial. At the same time, the new group sought to develop its own agenda.

Magín started to branch out throughout the country and soon counted a membership of about 400 women.[61] According to Norma Guillard, who kept Magín's records, the organization had 385 members in Havana and small chapters in two provinces, Pinar del Río and Santiago de Cuba.[62] From these data it is clear that Magín was essentially an urban phenomenon.

Magín's organizational development was supported by United Nations agencies, such as the United Nation's Children's Fund (UNICEF), the United Nations Development Program (UNDP), and the United Nations Fund for Women (UNIFEM).[63] The international aid agency OXFAM Canada was particularly instrumental in providing support for Magín, whether it entailed the provision of office supplies or the financing of publishing projects.[64] Counting on this significant assistance, Magín "organized countless workshops and international exchanges with feminists from all around the world."[65] In a short time it obtained high international visibility and became an important point of contact for researchers and activists interested in gender issues.

Sujatha Fernandes has theorized on the potential negative impact of these international connections. Fernandes advances the thesis that "the professional nature of international exchanges, and the pressures to seek funding from advocacy-oriented international foundations, encouraged the women of Magín to form a network of relatively privileged women in the media, rather than to build a broader feminist movement."[66] Although international contacts and support did to some degree shape the development of the organization, it is important not to overstate this influence. Contrary to the experience of women's organizations in many other Latin American countries, including Nicaragua, El Salvador, and Guatemala, where groups were indeed fiercely competing with one another for international funding and many did refocus on service-related activities, Magín faced no competition for financial resources from other women's groups. The organizational focus—on communication and the media—was rooted in the personal interests of several founding members. Furthermore, Magín's potential to build a broader feminist movement was mostly a function of limited organizational capacity, the restricted space for autonomous organizing, and the organization's short existence.[67] There is hardly evidence that Magín's international contacts had a demobilizing impact, restricting the scope of the organization's activities.

The organization's growth coincided with a 1996 government crackdown on civil society organizations and government institutions that were considered to be potentially subversive because they were openly challenging established government policies in an effort to bring about reform. With the United States government seeking to strengthen Cuban civil society in an attempt to undermine the revolution, all independent activity that challenged the status quo in some form became suspect. Not surprisingly, once Magín began to develop an independent profile, it ran into problems with the FMC and the party apparatus.[68]

The official FMC position always advocated against a diversification of the women's movement. Federation policy reflected the call to unity emphasized by the regime. FMC official Alemañy affirmed this viewpoint: "The more the women's movement divides itself, the weaker it is, since so many little groups remain without national structures [and] have little strength in the community. When we make a proposal, the whole world hears us because we speak for the women of the country. We represent 84 percent of all women older than fourteen years."[69] The FMC was supportive when groups of women would meet that shared professional backgrounds as long as these meetings were held under the FMC umbrella. Alemañy summarized this policy:

For example, the women journalists have what is called the Journalism Gender Circle that works together with the federation, and we ourselves have proposed its creation. . . . There is a Committee of Scientific Women that also works in coordination with us. When they evaluate anything in one of their reunions, they come to the federation in search of guidance, so we may participate with them. . . . All these women are part of the federation. That is, due to their specialty, they share common interests, but all their work is coordinated with the federation.[70]

In September 1996 the leadership of Magín was called to a meeting with the Central Committee of the Communist party and told by Raúl Castro, the minister of defense, that it was being "deactivated."[71] Although Magín's members accepted this decision, they were very resentful and blamed the FMC for seeking to monopolize and hegemonize any attempts of independent women's organizing. Most of the original members carried on with their work. Being deprived of Magín's institutional framework, they continued to be Magíñeras in their respective spheres.

According to FMC officials, Magín was dissolved because it lacked official backing. Alemañy maintained that the collective "emerged in a moment when there was no institution that supported them."[72] Every new organization is required to register with the Ministry of Justice. In order to be granted NGO status, the organization must obtain a "negative certificate" from the ministry as proof that there is no other registered NGO pursuing a similar purpose. Further, it must obtain sponsorship from a "state reference institution which affirms that the establishment of the NGO is in its interest. The reference institution subsequently has the right to attend the NGO's board meetings and inspect its accounts to confirm it is carrying out its stated purpose."[73] These rules effectively gave the Women's Federation control over Magín's existence. Since it was illegal in Cuba to "duplicate" an existing organization—in this case the FMC—it was in the FMC's power to shut down the new organization.

From Magín's perspective, its problem with the authorities was rooted in the fact "that there was jealousy concerning the importance the group was gaining."[74] Thus, FMC concerns and suspicions held by government officials combined to work against Magín. Once Magín had been abolished, the federation supported the creation of a substitute that could be closely controlled. From the FMC's perspective, "Magín disappeared with the emergence of the Journalism Gender Circle that is supported by the Union of Writers and Artists (Unión de Artistas y Escritores, or UNEAC) and the Union of Cuban Journalists (Unión de Periodistas de Cuba, or UPEC). . . . It has more or less the same interests that Magín had."[75]

A sustained societal dialogue is key to moving toward substantive gender equality. An autonomous women's movement would have a central function in this process. Women have an important role to play, but they need to be given the institutional space to organize and develop an agenda independent from state and party influence. It is in this regard that the "deactivation" of Magín has been counterproductive.

Women's Role in the Mass Organizations

In addition to the FMC, there are seven other mass organizations in Cuba, representing workers, farmers, students, and the youth movement. They are an integral part of Cuban society and perform very important functions.[76] The status of women in these movements reflected the prevailing gender relations in Cuban society. Although women were an important part of all organizations, they rarely held leadership positions that carried significant power.

All mass organizations were organically linked to the party, although their degree of autonomy varied. ANAP, the farmers' movement, was a case in point. The Cuban Communist party itself had not yet been established when the revolutionary authorities decided to organize the small farmers in support of the revolution. In 1961 the Cuban farmers were called together in a Congreso Campesino (Peasant Congress). According to Orlando Lugo, ANAP's founding president, the decision to create ANAP was made at this meeting.[77] The newly created Institute of Agrarian Reform (INRA) was designated to coordinate this effort. Mavis Álvarez recounted the history of ANAP's founding: "The direction given by the Revolution to INRA was to collaborate, to cooperate with the campesinos, with all those peasant associations so they would organize themselves and strengthen themselves, in order for them to participate in the revolutionary process."[78] The creation of ANAP was part of a restructuring of society, permitting the newly organized sectors to act in support of the revolution while at the same time benefiting from revolutionary policies.

ANAP's president confirmed that the leadership of the mass organizations consisted of party militants, pointing to the case of his organization: "At the national level, we are all party militants. At the provincial level, the majority is. There could be an official that is not a militant, but this is the exception."[79] At the grassroots level, however, far fewer of ANAP's members—only about 10 percent—were also party members.[80] Thus, party membership was reserved to an elite, which controlled all important positions in the union movement or the other mass organizations.

The gender composition of the mass organizations indicated significant differences in the level of women's representation. Women were most active in the neighborhood committees and the union movement and had less visibility in ANAP. Table 2.1 shows a substantial increase in women's participation in the neighborhood committees at all levels. Whereas these committees can be seen as "service institutions" and thus as corresponding to the traditional societal image of the type of organization women should be active in, the Committees in Defense of the Revolution played a significant role in Cuban society. Most importantly, over the past decade women have increasingly taken on leadership roles, both at the local and the national level.

Table 2.1. Women's Participation in the Structures of the Committees in Defense of the Revolution (CDRs), 1992–1998

Structure	Percentage of Women		
	1992	1996	1998
National Coordination	7.7	16.7	35.3
Provincial Leadership	18.3	22.6	31.6
Municipal Leadership	28.1	29.5	40.6
Zone Committees	34.4	40.0	40.0
Block Committees	39.2	41.1	44.2

Source: CDR–Departamento de Organización

Table 2.2. Women's Participation in the Structures of the Cuban Workers Central (CTC), 1990–2000

Structure	Percentage of Women		
	1990	1996	2000
National Council	19.9	36.2	35.4
National Secretariat	22.2	25.0	24.6
National Committee	32.0	21.0	29.2
National Unions	22.9	33.3	40.2
Provincial Unions	29.4	37.6	43.1
Union Sections	49.9	50.5	51.9

Source: CTC–Departamento de Organización

Table 2.3. Women's Participation in the Structures of the National Association of Small Farmers (ANAP), 1992–1999

Structure and Members	Percentage of Women	
	1992	1999
National Bureau	18.1	15.4
Provincial Bureau	18.7	14.4
Municipal Bureau	15.3	16.0
Base Organizations	11.3	41.7
Presidents of CAI and CCS	1.0	1.8
Members	14.5	—

Source: ANAP–Informe del Departamento de Organización
Note: CAI–Cooperativa Agropecuaria (Agricultural Cooperative); CCS–Cooperativa de Crédito y Servicio (Credit and Service Cooperative)

Similar developments can be observed in the case of the union movement. Table 2.2 demonstrates that by 2000, women comprised more than half the union membership. Significantly, more that one-third of the leadership positions were held by women.

Women clearly faced greater hurdles in Cuba's rural sector. According to ANAP president Orlando Lugo, in 2003 women farmers comprised 17 percent of the membership and 23 percent of the leaders. Although the average of female membership in leadership structures could have been that high, the definition of "leader" here is too vague to provide an accurate sense of the decision-making power these women held. Interestingly, the latest comprehensive official data available indicated a slight decrease in female leadership both at the national and provincial level. Moreover, although women's participation in local unions had risen significantly, they were almost completely excluded from the key leadership positions of local cooperatives. In 1999 women were leading less than 2 percent of all cooperatives.

Lugo emphasized the challenge of changing gender relations in Cuba's rural sector:

Let me tell you frankly. The peasant sector is a *machista* sector. The peasantry is much too machista. If there is a sector where work needs to be done for the obligation to work for equality to be understood, that there should be no differences—except [a person's] sex—between a man and a woman, that the woman can also occupy any position, that a woman can be as useful as any man . . . if there is a sector where work needs to be done, it is in this sector. In general, the peasant is machista. Nevertheless, we have worked very hard to change this [situation], we have coordinated our work well with the Federation of Cuban Women. . . . We have made progress. It is not the same to go to a hospital where the majority of our doctors, our nurses, our personnel are women than to talk in a cooperative where people cut sugarcane, where there are tractors. It is not the same [challenge].[81]

In light of this difficult climate for women, it is significant that ANAP has been working actively and has had some success in changing local conditions. According to official data, in 2003 women headed more than thirty of ANAP's municipal structures. Lugo emphasized that this progress was related to the educational transformation taking place in the countryside. "Today's peasants in Cuba are no longer the illiterate peasants of forty-five years ago. I have now two thousand university graduates in our cooperatives; I have thirteen thousand technicians in my cooperatives; [and] I have many agricultural engineers heading the cooperatives."[82]

Indeed, Cuba has made significant progress since the 1959 revolution. Mavis Álvarez described the early years after the fall of the Batista regime:

> Women participated rarely in meetings. This was [considered] the men's domain, and if some women did go to the meetings—because some did—you saw them always seated in the back, in the last seats or stands, there in the corners. Very few dared to speak, to give an opinion in such meetings. We achieved this little by little, giving them tasks, giving tasks within the organizations and promoting them for [leadership] positions. This was not easy. . . . And, of course, women being in charge, women directing men, in these first peasant movements, was very difficult. ANAP contributed and, at the same time, ANAP found support in the revolutionary laws that did not exclude women at all.[83]

Contrary to the practice of many Latin American farmers' movements, ANAP did not have a women's secretariat to promote gender equality within the organization. Instead, the group mainstreamed gender. "The gender agenda is a part of our work agenda. It is not a specific front, but is a part of the content of the organization's [work]."[84] ANAP's policies reflected the impact of international efforts. Once Cuba permitted international aid organizations to operate more freely in the country, they assumed an important role in the struggle to advance women's rights in the rural sector. In 2003 Oxfam Canada, Hivos from Holland, as well as several Scandinavian aid agencies all sponsored ANAP projects that trained women for leadership positions in an effort to change gender relations in the Cuban countryside.

ANAP is one of several mass organizations to have implemented specific programs to strengthen women's participation with the help of donor agencies from Europe. Mavis Álvarez emphasized the importance of international aid: "One way to break inertia is that you go to a region and you start to act in a way that gives women greater participation. If you arrive with the resources to do this, it is a lot easier, and for this reason [development] cooperation has helped. . . . Women's presence, their participation, requires, whether they like it or not, to think with a gender focus in everything you do."[85]

Women in the Workforce

An important measure of women's advancement is the degree to which they have assumed leadership positions in the various economic sectors. During the Women's Decade (1976–85), the FMC focused on incorporating women into the workforce and sought to end discrimination against women in the workplace. Table 2.4 indicates that women's participation in leadership positions greatly in-

Table 2.4. Women's Participation in Leadership Positions, 1997 and 1999

Economic Sector	Percentage of Women	
	1997	1999
Industry	16.1	17.6
Construction	13.8	14.6
Agriculture	20.0	20.5
Transportation	15.3	12.6
Communications	48.3	54.9
Commerce	32.2	34.1
Science	29.4	27.3
Education	52.3	53.5
Health, Social Work, Sport and Tourism	42.2	42.3
Finance and Insurance	62.6	63.0
Administration	29.4	34.8

Source: Oficina Nacional de Estadísticas, *La ocupación civil en Cuba*, 1999

Table 2.5. Gender Composition of the Cuban Workforce and Percentage of Female and Male Leadership

Year	Women	Men	Female Leaders	Male Leaders
1980	32.4	67.6	5.4	10.7
1990	38.9	61.1	4.9	7.6
2000	37.6	62.4	6.6	8.7
2001	37.4	62.6	6.3	8.4
2002	37.7	62.3	6.7	12.0

Source: Echevarría, "Mujer, empleo y dirección en Cuba," 6

creased throughout the Cuban economy, particularly in the finance, communications and health sectors. Women represented about 60 percent of all technicians, professionals, and scientists.[86] Between 1980 and 2001, the number of women in leadership positions doubled.[87] While this is an indication that policies favoring women's access to leadership positions have worked, it is important to emphasize that such policies failed to significantly narrow the gender gap between female and male leaders as a percentage of the respective workforces.

As table 2.5 demonstrates, in 1980 women represented about one-third of the workforce. Of these women, 5.4 percent were considered to be "leaders." Men, on the other hand, were two-thirds of the labor force, and more than 10 percent of all male workers occupied leadership positions. Thus, twice as many men—10.7 percent—held leadership positions. This gap narrowed over the following two decades, but by 2002 it had widened again, being close to the 1980 level.

Cuban researcher Dayma Echevarría has argued that promotion policies in Cuba were based on the degree of technical and professional expertise someone

Table 2.6. Women's Participation in Leadership Positions, 2002

	Women	Men
Leaders	34.8%	65.2%
Professionals and Technical Workers	66.4%	33.6%
Higher Education Graduates	64.7%	35.3%

Source: Oficina Nacional de Estadísticas, *Panorama económico y social de Cuba, 2002*, taken from Echevarría, "Mujer, empleo y dirección en Cuba," 8

achieved. Thus, considering the gender composition of university graduates or of professionals and technicians, the gap between male and female leaders is remarkable. Men were twice as likely to advance to positions of greater decision-making power than women.

Table 2.6 shows that in 2002, women represented two-thirds of university graduates, professionals, and technicians but held only one-third of the leadership positions. In Echevarría's view, women's access to leadership positions reproduced the sexual division of labor.[88] Her qualitative study of promotion practices of business executives confirmed that "in general, women in leadership positions were clustered around 'second-in-command' positions (sub directors, vice-presidents) or they were at the second level of the command structure (heads of departments, groups, or brigades)."[89] Thus, only select women reached the top leadership positions. Significantly, the official data fail to define what a "leadership position" entails. Based on the presence of the glass ceiling that women who try to get into positions of political power encounter (the topic of chapter 4), one can safely assume that similar mechanisms operate in the Cuban workplace.

Conclusion

The Cuban record is most impressive in the area of social and economic rights for women. The revolutionary programs created after 1959 benefited women greatly. Women's legal rights, together with their access to education and health care, were expanded dramatically. In general, women moved from the private sphere of the household into public life. They were incorporated into the workforce and started to hold leadership positions, albeit at a significantly lower level. For Cuban women, these improvements in societal position were inextricably linked with the person of Fidel Castro, who consistently advocated for women's rights.

Changing gender relations, however, proved to be a challenge. The transformation of the status quo took place slowly, particularly in the countryside. Arguably, a more effective women's movement might have accelerated change. The policies instituted by Cuba's revolutionary government did not benefit the emergence of an autonomous women's movement. Whereas Cuba provided benefits to women in the social and economic sphere in a manner unprecedented in Latin America, an *unintended consequence* of these material improvements was the preemption of the emergence of revolutionary feminism. The Cuban Women's Federation state-assigned monopoly in mobilizing and representing women and its symbiotic relationship with the Communist party impeded autonomous development and reduced the FMC to mobilizing women in support of the revolutionary project. As Julie Shayne has argued, the subordination of women's strategic gender interests to the interests of the revolution—as defined by a small, mostly male elite—is the key factor explaining the absence of "a collective feminist consciousness."[90] Based on her research, Shayne reaches the conclusion that to the extent that a feminist consciousness does exist, it "is an unconscious one, not sufficient for energizing a revolutionary feminist movement."[91] This raises the provocative question whether Cuba will follow the path of Nicaragua, where a hundred flowers of the feminist movement bloomed only after the Sandinista government had lost power.

Karen Kampwirth (2004) has explored the relationship between the revolutionary government in Nicaragua and the women's movement and found important parallels between Sandinista Nicaragua and Fidelista Cuba. Kampwirth argues that AMNLAE, the Nicaraguan women's movement, was characterized by the same lack of autonomy under the revolutionary government (1979–90) that we have seen in the case of Cuba's FMC. In an ominous sign for Cuba, Nicaragua's official women's organization became moribund once its sponsor, the Sandinista government, was defeated. At the same time, however, an autonomous women's movement started to flourish. Furthermore, Kampwirth demonstrates that women's organizing in the postrevolutionary period was characterized by the "beginning of coalition building across partisan and class lines."[92]

In summary, there is recognition that the FMC has accomplished a lot for women. Yet Cuban feminists rightly assert that, "at the level of gender consciousness, the federation has done very little work, and it has effectively stymied the development of an autonomous women's movement."[93] Some of the organization's critics acknowledge that the FMC has started to heed the call for change, albeit only at the level of discourse. "Until very recently, the federation had a triumphalist discourse. That already in Cuba there was nothing left that needed fighting for, that there was nothing more that we needed to achieve. Starting a few years ago, however, and until the present, people began to discuss [in the FMC] that violence [against women] is continuing, that inequality persists, if not in the laws, in the worst of all places—in social conventions. Laws are one thing that can be changed rapidly, but customs cannot."[94] The key deficiency in the federation's discourse and work has been its overemphasis on legal achievements to the detriment of recognizing the need to focus more on changing traditional thinking in order to move toward substantive gender equality. The federation would benefit from the existence of alternative independent voices articulating women's interests, since this would force the FMC to constantly reassess its own agenda.

The Cuban Political System

Competing Visions of Democracy

Freedom only for the supporters of the government, only for the members of one party—
however numerous they may be—is not freedom at all. Freedom is always and exclusively
freedom for the one who thinks differently.

Rosa Luxemburg, *The Russian Revolution*

Polemics regarding Cuba's political system are as old as the revolution itself. The United States and several European governments consider Cuba a communist dictatorship. Most countries are more nuanced in their views but nonetheless tend to be critical. Several governments in Africa, Asia, and Latin America, however, view Cuba as a model to be emulated. Their perspective is shared by private citizens across the world who advocate an alternative to a global system dominated by neoliberal economic policies that frequently fail to deliver the basic needs people rightfully expect to be guaranteed by their governments.

Cuban officials, while insisting on the democratic nature of their political system, are the first to agree that their country is not a typical Western-style democracy. The Cuban government emphasizes the substantive nature of the revolutionary process, with its excellent health-care and education facilities, and criticizes the priority given to "formal, representative democracy," which focuses on competitive elections while neglecting social and economic democracy. It is one of the many ironies of history, however, that Cuba places more value on some aspects of formal political participation, such as maintaining the consistently high turnout that characterizes Cuban elections, than do the United States or other countries. In order to evaluate the Cuban model in a meaningful way, we need to understand the basic features of the Cuban political system.

In this chapter, I trace the development of the Cuban system of government. Cuba has evolved from a system purely based on revolutionary legitimacy to one that seeks to emulate some features of the representative model. I examine the role of the Cuban Communist party, discuss the question of pluralism, and assess the current state of Cuban civil society. Whereas most Cuban citizens have remained in a position of accommodation, there is a significant minority that openly defies the current regime.

The Evolution and Structure of Cuba's System of Government

Political leadership in the Cuban system of government is located in two major structures: the Communist Party of Cuba (PCC) and the Organs of People's Power (Órganos del Poder Popular, or OPP). Cuba is a one-party system, with party and state forming a symbiotic relationship. For example, Fidel Castro combines the positions of commander-in-chief of the armed forces, president of the Council of State, president of the Council of Ministers, and first secretary of the PCC in his person. Party and state share interlocking directorates. As in Castro's case, the top party officials also hold the most important jobs in government. The Cuban constitution clearly assigns the party a hegemonic role. Thus, the center of decision-making power is located in the party structures. The most important government bodies, on the other hand, are the Council of State, headed by Castro, and the working commissions of the Cuban Parliament. It is in these permanent commissions that the work of the legislature is done, since Parliament meets only twice a year for a few days.

In 1974 the Organs of People's Power, the current Cuban system of government, were initiated in Matanzas Province. This first election was considered experimental, a test for the country's redirection toward representative democracy. Two years later, in 1976, the process was institutionalized. The OPP are comprised of municipal and provincial assemblies and a national Parliament. The members of the National Assembly are elected in a direct vote. Contrary to the Western model, the Cuban voter is given no choice—apart from abstaining or voting invalid—since there is only one candidate for each seat in Parliament.

The changes in Cuba's government structures were codified in the 1976 constitution. The revised document was the result of an effort to "broaden the base of legal and political institutionalization in the early 1970s."[1] It greatly strengthened electoral democracy by instituting direct elections for People's Power assemblies at the municipal level. Elections to the provincial and national assemblies, however, were initially indirect. In the elections from 1976 to 1986, the deputies to the National Assembly were elected by the municipal assemblies. This was also the case for the delegates to the provincial assemblies during 1976-89. Similar to the local level, these delegates served for a period of two and a half years. Following the 1992 constitutional reform, however, the voting system was changed. Elections to the provincial and national assemblies were now direct, and in the case of the provincial assembly, the mandate was extended to five years.

The 1992 reforms were intended to make the system more effective and to restore public confidence in the National Assembly. What makes the reforms remarkable is the fact that Cuba broadened direct democracy at a time when the society was in an unprecedented economic crisis. The government had no certainty that it would be vindicated by the outcome of the direct, secret vote for the provincial and national assemblies. Indeed, there were signs of dissent. In Havana, abstention rates were estimated to have been as high as 20 percent.[2]

Jesús García, an authority on Cuba's government structures, who has served several terms on Poder Popular assemblies, both at the local and the national level, affirmed these legitimacy problems: "There came a moment when the indirect elections conspired against the legitimacy of the persons [that were elected]. In this moment we suggested bringing the election closer to the citizens . . . to strengthen the relationship between the voters and those elected."[3] According to a 1990 public opinion poll, the "deputies were trusted by 59.5 percent of the respondents, while 40.6 percent questioned the OPP's democratic value, and 51.4 percent believed it lacked authority to solve problems affecting them."[4]

In light of this criticism, it is interesting to note that the majority of Cuban citizens viewed their political system as democratic. An opinion poll conducted before the 1998 elections found that almost 90 percent of the respondents considered the Cuban political system to be *more* democratic than other regimes.[5] As Max Azicri has pointed out, this "response was highly favorable, indicating a wide support margin, even if the regime had inflated the numbers."[6]

Jesús García argued that the focus of the discussion on which political system is more "democratic" is misplaced. In his view, attention should be given instead to the participatory nature of the Cuban system. "I don't like it when we use [the reference] 'is the most democratic system in the world' in a speech. I would say 'participatory.' These are two different things. For me, there is democracy in the United States. What happens is, it is a democracy that represents *el Capital* (the interest of wealth and money). Ours is a different type of democracy; we represent different interests."[7] Regardless of the conception of democracy the average Cuban citizen held, the revolutionary government enjoyed strong domestic support. The legitimacy its citizens conferred on the government explained the longevity of the regime and was considerably more significant in the eyes of the authorities than any outside validation by the United States or the European Union.

Cuban officials emphasize the participatory nature of the country's election process and assert that the Communist party plays no role in it. Roberto Díaz, the minister of justice and head of the National Election Commission, recently elaborated the official perspective:

> The [main] characteristic of the Cuban electoral system, what distinguishes it from other electoral systems, is that the party [Communist Party of Cuba or PCC] does not participate in the election process from an institutional point of view. In other systems, multiparty systems, the parties nominate the candidates and make up the lists. . . . The great difference and the fundamental characteristic of our system is that it is the people who nominate the candidates.[8]

Eduardo Freire, the president of the National Candidate Commission, affirmed that "the principle that governs our democratic election process is that the people elect and the people nominate."[9] Whereas these statements are true in a purely technical sense, the party's influence in the election process is, of course, pervasive.

From the perspective of the Cuban government, the process is in the hands of the voters. While this is arguably true at the local level, at the regional and national level the nomination process is controlled by the government-run mass organizations, with the Cuban Confederation of Workers (CTC) playing the leading role.[10] Since the mass organizations have little to no autonomy from the party, the party does in fact control the election process for the regional and national assemblies. Nevertheless, party control over candidate nominations has diminished somewhat; for example, prior to 1992, the party officially nominated the president of the National Candidate Commission (CNC).[11]

The party also played a role in deciding the composition of the National Election Commission, which oversees the election process. Although the Council of State formally appointed the members of the commission, the Communist party is firmly in control of this body. For example, as of 2006, twelve members of the Politburo, the party's highest decision-making body, occupied seats on the council.[12]

The PCC emerged in 1965 out of the various organizations that had formed the revolutionary coalition which overthrew the Batista regime. The constituent groups of this coalition had previously been called the Organizaciones Revolucionarias Integradas (Integrated Revolutionary Organizations, or ORI). With the creation of the PCC, Cuba officially became a one-party state. Marta Harnecker, the renowned scholar of Marxism and spouse of the now deceased Comandante Manuel Piñeiro, commonly known as Barbarroja (Red

Beard), emphasized that the PCC was conceived as an answer to distinct Cuban needs:

> Here in Cuba, the [concept of] the single party system (partido único) is not an idea of Lenin, it is not socialism that brought the sole party. Instead it is an idea of [José] Martí. The idea is that confronted with the [U.S.] empire and confronted with the internal division in this country, which was one of the last to decolonize, the problem was to find a way to unite the Cuban patriots. I think that the understanding of the party here is this one, to keep the patriots united against the empire.[13]

John Kirk has pointed out that José Martí's thought is indeed a key to understanding current Cuban reality.[14] The hero of the Cuban independence movement, commonly viewed as "a democratic revolutionary who was becoming increasingly radical,"[15] greatly influenced the revolutionary leadership's understanding on how to confront the United States. Martí, who initially admired the colossus to the north, grew increasingly disillusioned with U.S. policies and became keenly aware "of the unfortunate implications that this conduct of the United States held for Latin America as a whole."[16]

Fidel Castro and his close associates have consistently argued that in order to confront this threat, Cuban society had to be unified. The Cuban Communist party, the vanguard of the revolutionary process, sought to lead the country by example in acting with one voice. While the Cuban revolution has arguably survived the many threats it has faced from the United States because of being able to present a united front, the need for unity has, on the other hand, impeded the development of a truly pluralist society.

The party exercised its influence over society through the mass organizations. As discussed in the previous chapter, the leadership of the mass organizations was composed of party militants. The symbiotic relationship between the mass organizations and the party extended to the government structures. Max Azicri has noted that the fusion between party and state structures is inherent in the system and needs to be evaluated as such:

> The OPP's [Organs of People's Power] independence and democratic nature has been questioned, as has the control the PCC exercises over it. It is debatable whether the OPP and PCC could coexist without infringing upon each other and whether a deputy could shed party affiliation and represent his or her constituency in the case of dual membership. Hence, if the OPP stands for democracy, is Cuban socialism truly democratic? No matter how central these questions are to liberal democracy, they are not germane to the organic structure of a socialist political system.[17]

Nevertheless, it is essential to establish the weaknesses and strengths of the Popular Power model, albeit on Cuban terms. Although Cuba initiated a process of incorporating features of representative government into its system, in the final analysis, power continued to be located in the Communist party. Carollee Bengelsdorf maintained that "the extreme overlap between party membership and delegate status [results] . . . in a huge gap between theoretical functioning and actual reality."[18] We need to keep this reality in mind when examining how the system operated at the local and national level.

Municipal Level

Voter participation in the selection process of candidates to the local assemblies has traditionally been very high. According to official data, in the 1976 elections 77 percent of the registered voters participated in the meetings held to select the candidates to the municipal assemblies. Participation reached its highest point in 1984 with 91 percent and has since then remained around 85 percent.[19] Only during the height of the Cuban economic slowdown in 1992 did less than 80 percent of the voters attend these grassroots meetings.

At the local level, each municipal assembly delegate represents a small geographical area of a few city blocks. This electoral district is divided into seven nomination areas, with the intention of facilitating citizen input into the candidate nomination process.[20] Thus, the neighbors of a city block or a hamlet come together to nominate their candidates for the local assemblies. Candidates are primarily chosen based on the reputation and public profile they enjoy in the neighborhood. Depending on the neighborhood's size, a minimum of two and a maximum of eight candidates are nominated for each municipal council seat. As I discuss below, the electoral rules for local elections make women candidates susceptible to traditional gender views, which prioritize male leadership.[21]

These exercises in grassroots democracy sometimes led to unconventional results. National Assembly president Ricardo Alarcón told of a case where the political counsel of the Canadian embassy was nominated by his neighbors:

He participated so much [in neighborhood activities] that he was proposed as a candidate, a delegate for his neighborhood. . . . He went to all the meetings, including those at which the delegate rendered accounts. In the meetings there in the neighborhood, he was well known. The people saw him. When they nominated him, it was because he was a type that the people considered an active neighbor. . . . [When the Canadian was nominated in the end, he told his neighbors, flattered and stunned:] "But I can't [be a candidate], I am the counsel of the Canadian embassy."[22]

Until 1992 the members of the provincial and national parliaments were selected in indirect elections by the members of the municipal councils. Ricardo
Alarcón, president of the National Assembly, initially opposed the change to
institute direct elections for these bodies, arguing that the town councils were
more effective in exercising a control function than the electorate in general.
He subsequently changed his mind.[23]

The rendering of accounts was an important feature of the Cuban system,
and a considerable number of deputies were recalled. Peter Roman has pointed
out that the systematic process of delegate accountability is considered a distinguishing feature of the Cuban political system.[24] Roman, who witnessed
several accountability sessions, observed constituents vigorously questioning
their delegates. The sessions were also a means to keep citizens engaged in the
political process.[25]

National Level

At the national level, the National Candidate Commission (Comisión Nacional de Candidaturas, or CNC) oversees the process of selecting candidates.[26]
Under the 1992 election system, there is only one candidate for each provincial
or national parliamentary seat. Thus, voters are not choosing between competing candidates, instead they vote for one or more of the candidates on the
slate selected by the candidate commissions and confirmed by the municipal
assemblies. As we will see, this system of candidate selection benefits female
candidates.

It is a main argument of this chapter that the Cuban National Assembly dif-
fers from other parliaments in important regards. President Alarcón outlined
these differences:

> One of the most important is the fact that, with some exceptions, among
> them myself, it is not a professional Parliament. The majority of the
> deputies have a function in society which is not one of being a politician,
> that is to say a professional politician, dedicated to fulfill a task in the
> Parliament for which he receives income, a salary. This is not the case
> for the majority of the Parliament. The composition of the assembly also
> has to do with this phenomenon. Almost one-half [of the deputies] are
> also municipal assembly delegates who are also not professionalized,
> with the exception of those that are municipal assembly presidents or
> presidents of a *consejo popular* [an administrative unit that represents
> several neighborhoods].[27]

Members of the National Assembly continue to exercise their original profession held at the time of their election and receive their original salary. Ac-

cording to the constitution, "the deputies receive the same salary or pay of their workplace and maintain, in all regards, their ties with it."[28] The rationale behind this provision was to ensure that no one seeks to serve in the legislature or in a municipal council because it would be attractive from an economic point of view. Leonardo Martínez, the president of the Commission for Productive Activities, arguably the Parliament's most influential standing commission, emphasized the altruistic nature of holding a mandate in Parliament: "Thus, this interest [in material gain] does not exist in someone who wants to become a deputy." No one seeks this position "because it might get him a better salary, a car, a house, or I don't know what. It will get him nothing. What it will get him is more work."[29]

A greatly increased workload was indeed the reality for those National Assembly members who served on the legislature's working commissions. Deputies who held such appointments had little or no time to exercise their original profession. This made voters at the neighborhood level reluctant to "give up" a treasured professional to serve in the Parliament. Ana María Moreno, the head of the Health, Sports, and Environment Commission of the National Assembly, affirmed this. When she was elected, the neighborhood lost its family doctor. Thus, after serving her five-year term, the voters refused to renominate her. According to Moreno, her constituents had vowed from the very beginning: "She is going to be there for five years but we will get her back."[30] The voters did not change their views, and once Moreno had completed her initial term, they did not nominate her as a candidate for the 2003 elections.

The neighborhood's reaction highlighted the relative lack of power and influence attributed to a member of Parliament. A physician's services were considered invaluable in the eyes of the neighborhood, compared to having a member of the community serve in Parliament. The Cuban experience was in stark contrast to the prestige parliamentary service confers in other countries. Even the select group of Cuban parliamentarians who served on the standing committees and whose work made them more comparable to their counterparts in other countries were obviously not viewed as being able to deliver "legislative pork" to their constituents.

Although the Cuban model ensured that the members of the National Assembly remained in touch with the Cuban people, the downside was a lack of legislative expertise. Even among the members of the working commissions, only the leaders were professionals in the sense that they worked full-time as parliamentarians. "In the year 1992," Leonardo Martínez affirmed, "one began to professionalize a minimum group of indispensable deputies in order to carry out the work of the commissions in Parliament, because we realized that we really needed someone here in the offices that would coordinate the work of the commission. For example, in our commission, which consists of forty deputies, I am the only professional."[31] According to Martínez, in 2003 the National Assembly had only eight professionals among its deputies, and three of them were women.

Alarcón argued that the lack of professionals with expertise in the traditional areas of legislative responsibilities, be it agriculture, finance, defense, health care, or education, could be compensated for if the assembly's working commissions were to draw on the expertise available throughout Cuba. These "people's advisers" would not be paid, of course. Alarcón joked that he would be "kicked out" of Parliament were he to present a budgetary request for salary to compensate such people's advisers for their services.[32]

I would argue that the issue here only partially concerned technical expertise or knowledge. More importantly, since the majority of the deputies were not full-time politicians and often lacked a solid understanding of how the system was supposed to work, their actual power and influence within the Cuban system of government was limited. Although, according to the constitution, "the assembly is the highest organ of power,"[33] in reality the legislature had a diminished status. Indeed, a knowledgeable insider, Jesús García, acknowledged that, "day to day, it is the Council of Ministers that takes the decisions. How does one guarantee that this highest organ of power [the assembly] is truly the highest organ of power if the other one takes the daily decisions? It is guaranteed to the extent that the commissions function well."[34]

The National Assembly met only twice a year for a few days. Ten permanent commissions conducted the daily work of the legislature. It is in these commissions that new law projects were elaborated. The commissions also served a control function, conducting social and economic impact studies that sought to confirm whether decisions taken by the National Assembly or the Council of State had actually been implemented.[35]

When Parliament is not in session, it is represented by the Council of State. The National Assembly elects the members of the council from among its membership. In theory, the council had the power to charge the permanent commissions with their respective agendas. In practice, however, the assembly's president led and coordinated the work of the commissions.[36]

It is in the Council of State where legislative power is located. Although the president of the National Assembly was not a de jure member of the council, in practice he was very much a part of it. According to Alarcón, however, "logically, the person who presides over the National Assembly, and, by extension, he who replaces him, the vice president, are, in fact, de officio members."[37] Indeed, Alarcón affirmed that he was consulted whenever the council took a decision and "when I take a long time in responding they complain. . . . I am being treated equal to any other member of the council. I am certain that I consider myself a member of the Council of State. I have stopped it [the work of the council] because I had an opinion, I did not agree."[38]

There is general agreement that the stature of the assembly was greatly enhanced when Ricardo Alarcón assumed its presidency. Jesús García conveyed the extremely positive image many Cubans have of Alarcón's leadership: "One notes a change in the work of the assembly starting with the presidency of Alarcón. I would say that there are two phases [before and after Alarcón]. Also it is a [new] phase of maturity. . . . In recent years the work of the commissions has matured."[39] Thus, the assembly was starting to assert itself and assume the role ascribed to it by the constitution.

The Question of Pluralism

From the Cuban point of view, pluralism is encouraged. Cuban officials argued, however, that the commonly held view, which identifies pluralism with a multiparty system, was inappropriate. In their view, such a definition indicated a conceptual understanding that was limiting. Alarcón summarized the Cuban position succinctly:

> I defend pluralism as a fundamental concept. Now, what I reject is the intent of some to identify pluralism with a multiparty system. They are distinct things. Pluralism is something that is not easy to achieve. It requires a transformation, including of people's consciousness. . . . It is difficult in a society to achieve real, direct, effective participation of the people, of the government, in all its diversity. This is pluralism. . . . Those who want to equate this with multiparty politics are really limiting pluralism. They are trying to pigeonhole it, to reduce it to an appearance of diversity. . . . Those who defend representative democracy like a dogma—at the core of this is the intent to reduce the idea of democracy to one of its formal aspects. . . . The essence of the question has never focused on this but on how to achieve that the people, the citizens, be the protagonists in the exercise of power. This is very easy to say, and it is apparently resolved [in representative democracies] with periodic elections in which the people go and choose. But in the end [they choose] between candidates although they had no real capacity to influence who would be the candidates. In our system there is a much truer capacity for this. No one can be a candidate without having been nominated, be it by the people directly or by the people's representatives.[40]

Thus, from a Cuban perspective, their system guaranteed real citizen input in the selection of candidates, whereas candidates in most Western democracies are chosen either by the party hierarchy or need substantial financial resources to promote their campaigns. Ana María Moreno proudly noted the distinguishing characteristics of the Cuban system:

> We are accused of lacking democracy, but I think that the Cuban democratic model is very transparent. In other countries, in order to become a deputy or a senator, one needs to have money in the first place or you have to be supported by and financed by a specific group of people that has money. . . . Our case is different. I am here representing the people that elected me, and I don't receive a cent for this.[41]

Nevertheless, the Cuban system has its own restrictions and limitations for anyone who opposes the established system of government. When asked to what degree the system permitted members of the opposition to participate, Roberto Díaz, the minister of justice, insisted:

> Someone who is not with the revolution enjoys equal rights from an electoral point of view to nominate [a candidate] in a nomination assembly and to vote. Equal conditions, and if there were a majority of these people in an electoral district, by law, by the electoral procedures, they could put up their candidate. They could nominate their candidate [and] could elect their representative as a delegate to the municipal assembly. What happens is that the revolution counts with the majority, with the immense, overwhelming majority of the people. Thus, according to the electoral rules, an enemy of the revolution could get into any of these positions. If it does not happen, it is because the people crush them—the people—not the army, not the police.[42]

The minister of justice was correct in asserting that, theoretically, a dissident could get elected. In practice, however, this was close to impossible. The system required that the majority of the voters in a particular neighborhood, would be opposed to the government, would unite behind a specific opposition candidate and would feel comfortable in supporting a dissident in such a neighborhood forum. People in the neighborhood would be concerned about gaining negative national attention by electing an opposition candidate. Even if this were to occur, the opposition candidate would be one delegate among many on the municipal council with little to no influence over policy-making. At the regional and national level, additional hurdles were to be overcome: the mass organizations and the Candidate Commissions. It is unlikely that a dissident would be nominated as a pre-candidate by a mass organization and equally improbable that he or she would appear among the final list of candidates presented to the municipal council by the Candidate Commission or be approved once presented.[43]

García acknowledged that the election procedures at the regional and national level functioned as protective barriers, insulating the regime from oppositional challenges: "I do not deny it. Technically speaking and in the clearest language, I would say that scientifically it is indisputable that they are almost protective mechanisms of our democracy regarding whom we are going to elect. But this is the mechanism of our democracy. The mechanism of the democracy in the United States is that one needs to have millions of dollars in order to be a candidate."[44] García had a point. A candidate who is not affiliated with an established party in the European Union or the United States faces staggering odds in any effort to get elected. In addition, in the United States, candidates need substantial personal wealth and/or special fundraising skills to have a chance at being elected. However, these countries have competitive party systems with at least two viable parties, giving the voter at least nominally a choice, albeit limited. From the Cuban perspective, the voters can choose between different candidates at the local level. From a Western perspective, however, it is the monopoly of the Communist party that eliminates choice a priori. Most significantly, it is the noncompetitive nature of the national elections that presents a democratic deficit.

Although Cuba is a one-party state, not all elected representatives belong to the PCC. Citizens that are elected to serve in Parliament are not necessarily party members. At times, deputies will join the Communist party after having been elected. A case in point is assembly member Ana María Moreno: "I became a militant in May 1999. First I became a deputy. When I became a deputy, I was not a party militant, but afterward I joined the party."[45] According to Cuban officials, about 85 percent of all members of Parliament are party members.[46]

Alarcón emphasized that the question of pluralism should not be reduced to electoral politics. He advocated a pluralist society with a proliferation of divergent views in all aspects of life. Most observers would agree that Cuba has a long way to go before it reaches such a state of affairs. The focus on national unity stifles any expression of dissent, even when it comes in the form of constructive criticism voiced by supporters of the revolution. These limitations are recognized and resented by many citizens:

> The pluralism that we need is not the one prescribed to us, of a multitude of parties, but rather pluralist debate within the party of the revolution. We need more grassroots pluralist discussion among those organized in the revolution and more in the media. There's a lot to debate, because there are many different views within the revolution about controversial

topics. It's not enough to debate in the National Assembly. No matter how representative our representatives are, the debate should be broad, public, within all society, even if many people say stupid things. That's how it starts.[47]

Cuba lacks a broad array of media and open discussions in the workplace, in the universities, and in similar settings, which are essential to facilitate this sort of vibrant debate. María López Vigil insisted in the late 1990s that the "issue of the media is not a minor one. It goes to the very heart of Cuban political practice, which, more than party pluralism, needs a plurality of opinions, of voices—an authentic diversity. The media problem is long-standing, but today, when Cubans' social consensus regarding the revolutionary project is undergoing such a severe crisis, it becomes central."[48] In her view, Cuban society lacks an authentic "culture of debate."[49]

The Unity Vote

The Cuban election system is criticized due to the lack of competition among candidates at the provincial and national level. Under the 1992 election system, there is only one candidate for each provincial or national parliamentary seat. Thus, voters are not choosing between competing candidates; instead, they vote for one or more of the candidates on the slate selected by the candidate commissions and confirmed by the municipal assemblies. Alarcón maintained that Cuba chose such a noncompetitive system in order to avoid "politicking, competition and division."[50]

Not only is there a lack of competition between candidates with opposing ideological views, but Cuban authorities strongly encourage the electorate to vote for the entire slate of candidates established by the Candidate Commission, in a policy called the "unity vote." The official rationale states that this ensures that incumbents do not enjoy an undue advantage due to their greater name recognition.[51] Fidel Castro has been an effective advocate for the unity vote in every election since 1992. In 2003 more than 90 percent of the voters exercised the unity vote option. Apart from the electorally insignificant Isle of Youth, where 15 percent chose the selective vote, the City of Havana had the highest incidence of selective voting with 12 percent.[52] Alarcón justified the unity vote this way:

> We ask the people that they vote for all [candidates]. I can tell you about my experience. . . . In all areas of District 2 of Plaza [an electoral division of Havana where Alarcón stood for election], I obtained a vote substantially higher than the two *compañeros* who are part of the candidate list for deputy. . . . I am the most known, more than the president of

the town council who is well known in the town by the people in the municipal government, and a *compañero* who is very good and is also a neighborhood delegate who is well known in his neighborhood. . . . The people that choose the selective vote do not vote for all three but for one or two [of the candidates]. The overwhelming majority of the non-unity votes are for me, and there is no doubt that from the point of view of electoral politics, the votes that these *compañeros* received I helped to bring about.[53]

Thus, voters who supported Alarcón, a highly respected, key government official, and chose to vote for the entire slate of candidates simultaneously supported lesser-known candidates of local stature. The unity vote also favored gender and racial equality as well as younger candidates. Voters who exercised the unity vote could not opt to discriminate against candidates simply because of their gender, race, or age. Alarcón considered this an important advantage:

> In spite of years of socialism, in spite of a lot of democracy and everything you want, there are those that hold discriminatory views toward women—one of the three [candidates on the ballot] is a woman. There are those with [discriminatory views] of the racial type—the neighborhood candidate is a mulatto. One woman and one mulatto, both of them young, both of them much younger than I am—in some [voters] one finds prejudice against young people. There is the tendency of people to believe that they should vote for the one that has what the Americans call "name recognition."[54]

In short, Alarcón argued convincingly that the unity vote was advantageous for "less established candidates." From the regime's point of view, the unity vote ensures that the social engineering of the Candidate Commission cannot be undone by voters choosing among candidates according to their individual preferences and prejudices. On the other hand, the pressure on the electorate to give up their right to be selective in their vote limits the citizens' democratic right to exercise freely their right to choose.

Cubans are proud that personal wealth and resources or the ability to raise campaign funds is not a factor in deciding who gets elected to Parliament. Open competition between candidates, albeit from the same party, would benefit those with greater resources. Campaigning "at the level of the higher structures is impossible without an apparatus [of support]. These two *compañeros*, in particular the mulatto, have no means to wage a campaign throughout Vedado [a neighborhood in Havana]. He has no car, he has no secretary, he has no telephone."[55] Thus, such a candidate would not be competitive against the president of the National Assembly or any other established national figure.

Civil Society: Accommodation and Opposition

From the Cuban perspective, the core of civil society is represented by the eight official mass organizations. As discussed earlier, however, these grassroots organizations are not independent actors, although they are officially considered to be nongovernmental organizations. Thus, a key question to be addressed when one evaluates the Cuban political system is whether autonomous societal organizations exist.

According to Roberto Díaz, the minister of justice, 2,254 nongovernmental associations had registered with the ministry by the end of 2002.[56] Indeed, there has been an explosion of NGOs over the past decade. Gillian Gunn has argued that "Cuba's NGOs grew because the government deemed them useful financial intermediaries and because citizens desired self-help organizations capable of resolving local problems the state was unwilling or unable to address."[57]

In the wake of the Soviet Union's demise, the government needed to capture alternative financial resources. Hard-pressed for new sources of income, "Cuban authorities therefore permitted a few ministries to establish parallel NGOs and re-labeled as 'NGOs' some existing mass organizations and think tanks formerly associated with the Central Committee bureaucracy."[58] In addition to these "official NGOs," hundreds of grassroots organizations emerged, representing a gamut of interests, including religious, environmental, and cultural constituencies.

The Cuban government maintains an ambivalent relationship with NGOs. They are encouraged because they can contribute to the alleviation of the persuasive financial problems but are viewed with suspicion for their potential to act as Trojan horses for U.S. interests. Undeniably, it is the official policy of the U.S. government to strengthen Cuban civil society in an attempt to undermine the revolution. Thus, any independent activity that could be interpreted as challenging the status quo in some form was viewed with concern by the authorities. Over the past fifteen years, periods of civil society growth have alternated with times when Cuban authorities sought to restrict independent groups. For example, a period of liberalization ended abruptly in March 1996, when a government crackdown affected opposition organizations and independent groups, including official research and think tanks such as the Center for the Study of America (Centro de Estudios sobre América, or CEA).

Under the 1985 law that governed the registration of NGOs, no group could be registered if its goals violated the constitution. This stipulation effectively impeded the registration of political parties since the constitution proclaimed a one-party state. Under the Associations Law, Cuban authorities had considerable discretion in rejecting the application of any group. The provisions of the law barred groups "whose activities could prove damaging to social interests" or "whose applications demonstrate the impossibility of attaining their proposed objectives."[59]

According to Gunn, "Human rights organizations have been denied registration on the grounds that they are covert political parties."[60] The discussed provisions made it extremely difficult for organized opposition activities to emerge. Despite these restrictions, a number of organized dissident groups operated throughout the island, although they were not legally registered. European diplomats confirmed in 2003 that compared to earlier periods, the government had given dissidents considerable maneuvering room. For example, members of opposition groups visited with European Union embassy officials on a regular basis and sent out communiqués via electronic mail and fax. An important recent effort of organized dissent was the Varela project. It gained national and international attention on the occasion of former U.S. president Jimmy Carter's 2002 visit to Cuba.

The Varela Project

In May 2002 organizers of the Varela project delivered to the National Assembly boxes of petitions bearing more than eleven thousand signatures. According to a copy of the actual petition, it entailed a legal initiative for a referendum on the Varela project, which consisted of five key proposals: guarantees of the right to freedom of speech and association, amnesty for political prisoners, the right for Cuban citizens to create enterprises, and a new electoral law.[61] Some analysts saw the petition as a window of opportunity for reform, since it advocated change while doing so within Cuba's prevailing legal framework. Described in a U.S. press report as "the boldest challenge to President Fidel Castro's Communist government in more than 40 years,"[62] the fate of the project was in limbo until January 24, 2003.

On that day, a Cuban legislative committee denied that the petition should go forward. Miguel Álvarez, a senior aide to Ricardo Alarcón, presented the official view: "The case was reviewed by the Constitutional and Legal Affairs Committee, which decided not to proceed, and to inform its sponsors of that verdict."[63] The grounds of the decision were not elaborated on. Eduardo Lara, who served as the principal adviser to the National Assembly's Commission of Constitutional and Juridical Matters, explained in a 2002 interview that

Cuban officials had interpreted the aims of the petition as seeking to amend the constitution.[64] This interpretation provided Cuban officials with a technical reason that justified the government's refusal to review the petition.

The Varela project was introduced by its sponsors under Article 88 of the Cuban constitution. This constitutional provision also gives the power to propose a new legal initiative to the citizens. It stipulates that in case of a citizen-sponsored initiative, "it is the indispensable prerequisite that the initiative is exercised by at least 10,000 citizens that have voting rights."[65] Although the sponsors of the petition had a sufficient number of signatures, fulfilling the formal constitutional requirement for a citizen initiative, the government objected on substantive grounds. In its view, Article 88 did not apply in the case of the Varela project, since the petition aimed at modifying the constitution itself, which is a prerogative reserved for the National Assembly.[66]

The Varela initiative attracted worldwide attention, and Oswaldo Payá, its main sponsor, became a celebrity. His contributions to peaceful change were recognized by several international organizations and governments, which awarded him prestigious human rights awards. Payá did not receive permission to fly to the United States to receive the W. Averell Harriman Democracy Award in September 2002. He was allowed to travel to Europe, however, to personally accept the European Parliament's Sakharov Prize in December 2002. During his fifty-day trip, Pope John Paul II received Payá, and, passing through the United States, he met with Colin Powell, then secretary of state. Before returning to Cuba, Payá also met with leaders of the Cuban exile community in Miami.[67] No stranger to controversy, he angered many expatriates by advocating an end to the U.S. embargo.

It is interesting that Payá enjoyed celebrity status in human rights circles of the United States and Europe, whereas he had limited stature in Cuba and the substance of the Varela project remained virtually unknown on the island, even after President Carter brought the initiative to national attention. Carter discussed the project in a public meeting that was broadcast live on Cuban television. The May 2002 event was watched by millions of Cuban television viewers, and all of them heard the exchange between President Carter and the dean of the University of Havana's Law School concerning the Varela petition. Yet in the months following this televised exchange, most Cubans and even intellectuals who tended to be well informed did not know the content of the petition. This indicated either a lack of interest for the Varela project or the ability of the government to control the dissemination of information associated with dissident activities. Interestingly, a select group of people—those with Internet access—was better informed. Technology has started to change the degree to which the government is able to control the flow of information, a reality affirmed by several sources: "It appears that very few people know of it [the Varela project]. I got it through electronic mail. However, it is true, it is not in the public domain."[68]

Cuban government officials differed in their reactions when asked about the Varela project. The minister of justice professed ignorance when asked in November 2002 about the reforms proposed by the project: "I don't know it. I am unaware of it. That is, I don't know the project as such."[69] While Roberto Díaz showed great reluctance to get into a discussion concerning the Varela proposal, other government officials, including Ricardo Alarcón, freely discussed the project's merits. The Varela initiative was definitely considered a significant challenge by the revolutionary authorities, as evidenced by the government's actions once the Varela plan had been publicized nationally.

Enshrining "Socialism" in the Constitution

In June 2002, the month following President Carter's visit and at a time of threatening statements by the Bush administration, the government mobilized Cuban citizens to show their support for the regime. Preempting any initiative to change the political nature of the government, "socialism" was to be enshrined in the constitution. According to the official version presented by the minister of justice, the constitutional change initiated with the June 2002 referendum "was an initiative of the mass organizations" to incorporate into the constitution "the irrevocability of the socialist character of our political system."[70]

For three days, while Cuban voters had the opportunity to sign the referendum, the country went on official holiday and came to a standstill. In every city block and rural area, voters could sign the petition. Whereas neighbors appeared to notice who signed, opposition to the initiative was formally accepted. Ana María Moreno, a member of Parliament, affirmed:

> People approached me and said: "I am not going to sign. I do not agree that socialism should be irrevocable." "Oh, this is your reason." "Is there a book [one can sign] in order to say no?" I told him: "No, he who does not say yes, says no. He who abstains does the same." Some people said: "Am I obliged to sign?" "No [I said]. You are not obliged to sign." "Will I have a problem if I don't sign?" "No [I assured them]. You won't have a problem if you don't sign."[71]

Most independent observers, including many Cubans, viewed the referendum as a response to the challenge posed by the Varela petition and the threats issued by the Bush administration. A former local government official shared her view on this subject:

The purpose has been to give an answer in light of all the threats received by the United States government, such as Bush considering us one of the countries on the list of terrorist nations, and all the other threats and public denunciations, such as [accusing us of] possessing biological weapons and all these other things that happened. Well, I think we tried to give an answer on how the Cuban people think of this revolution, its president, its government, [and] its party.[72]

At the end of June, the Cuban government announced that it had collected signatures from 98.97 percent of Cubans for the petition seeking to declare the current system as "untouchable." On June 27, 2002, the National Assembly ratified the constitutional changes with the unanimous support of the deputies. A Western observer might look at such figures with incredulity. However, those that maintain that these figures were fabricated are mistaken. Cubans regarded support for this referendum as their patriotic duty. Sonnia Moro shared her view of the common citizen's thinking: "I think that one of the strongest sentiments that Cubans share is their patriotism. The motivation of the people who voted may differ from one to the next. However, I think that the foremost motivation is that the aggression of a foreign power forces us to make decisions.... You cannot force a country of eight million voters."[73]

The country continued in turmoil in the months following the referendum. James Cason, the head of the U.S. Interest Section, engaged in a series of high-profile activities intended to show the support of the Bush administration for the opposition movement. The United States has the largest foreign delegation in Cuba despite the fact that the two countries have no diplomatic relations. In the spring of 2003, the country had experienced a wave of airplane and boat hijackings. The Cuban authorities responded to the perceived threat to internal security in April 2003. The day before the government crackdown, Alarcón freely acknowledged the degree to which the Cuban authorities were aware of the opposition's plans:

If we have managed to infiltrate *compañeros* [sent there by the Cuban government] into those groups in Miami, can anyone doubt our capacity to put *compañeros* into their groups here within [Cuba]? I can assure you that apart from the declassified information, the other great source of our information are these groups themselves. We know what the American [U.S. envoy James Cason] tells them in the meetings, we know the resources they are given, we know the techniques they use to hide them. The information is up-to-date and plentiful. . . . What they have achieved is little.[74]

Dozens of dissidents were rounded up throughout the country and sentenced to long prison terms. A total of twenty-nine trials were held throughout Cuba, with the sentences ranging from six to twenty-eight years. In the appendix, I present a list of the citizens that were arrested, the length of their sentence, and their place of regional origin.

According to Oswaldo Payá, 40 percent of the signatories of the Varela petition were female.[75] Since many of the dissidents who received prison sentences, including Luis Enrique Ferrer (who received the longest sentence), were affiliated with the Varela project, one would expect to find several women among the arrested dissidents. Yet among the seventy-five members of the opposition who were sentenced, Martha Beatriz Roque was the only woman. What makes the gender composition of those sentenced even more noteworthy is the fact that three of the seven arrested opposition members who turned out to be state security agents were women.

In light of the lack of corroborating data, we can only speculate on whether government officials considered female supporters of the opposition to be less of a threat. Similarly, it appears that prevailing gender views—as was the case during the revolutionary struggle—continued to give women an advantage when working undercover. There is significant evidence that images of women are increasingly used by both the government and the opposition in an effort to manipulate public opinion and to gain strategic advantages. For example, following the spring 2003 crackdown, a group of women whose husbands were part of the seventy-five prisoners organized weekly protests as the "Ladies in White" staging candlelight vigils in an effort to garner attention. In response, the Federation of Cuban Women mobilized its members in a show of support for the Castro government. In 2005, the two sides engaged in public confrontations.[76]

As Alarcón intimated, Cuban state security had indeed thoroughly infiltrated the opposition. During the course of the trial, seven dissidents, among them several high-profile opposition figures, acknowledged that they were government agents. For example, journalist Néstor Baguer, an iconoclastic opposition figure who headed the Association of the Independent Press of Cuba, announced under questioning by the judge that he had served Cuban state security as agent "Octavio" since 1960! Similarly, Odilia Collazo, known in her role as the president of the Party for Human Rights of Cuba, responded when asked whether she was a member of the opposition: "In reality, I am not a member of the opposition. Today, I have the privilege to tell you that I am, precisely, one of the people chosen by the Cuban government, by the Ministry of Interior [to infiltrate the opposition]. Today, I am showing the whole world that I am an agent, agent Tania."[77]

Observers were perplexed by the fact that the Cuban government revealed the degree to which it had infiltrated the opposition over the years and by so doing destroyed an effective network that had been built over decades. The high number of agents among those arrested was proof to many that the old adage concerning the Cuban opposition was correct: "One third Cuban agents, one third CIA agents, and one third opposition." Among the last third were people who truly opposed the government as well as a number of opportunists who sought to be recognized as opposition figures in order to obtain material rewards, including being able to emigrate to the United States.

Government officials and many Cuban citizens did not view the people who were arrested as bona fide dissidents. Orlando Lugo, a member of the Council of State, affirmed:

No self-respecting country in the world would permit what this Mister of the U.S. Interest Section did—to create counterrevolutionary groups without scruples. They are not dissidents. They are counterrevolutionaries at the service of the CIA. Everyone in the world knows this. Also, they are not journalists. Four of them have a university degree in journalism, the others are CIA workers, paid by the [U.S.] Interest Section.[78]

Regardless of how one views the people arrested—as dissidents or as counterrevolutionaries—their sentences were excessively harsh. Yet another group's actions were considered to deserve even more severe punishment. At about the same time, the authorities arrested the hijackers of a ferryboat who had attempted to divert the boat to the United States. This group received different treatment since its members were not considered dissidents and the majority had a criminal background. Three of the hijackers were executed because "they were the ones that organized the assault. They were the leaders, those who got the weapons, premeditated the assault, and were conscious of the consequences. They were the protagonists whereas the others were the companions."[79]

Many ordinary Cuban citizens rejected the imposition of the death penalty and the haste with which it was carried out. International reaction was also negative. The European Union held the view that "the summary trial and rapid execution of [the] three hijackers were carried out in breach of international minimum standards for the implementation of the death penalty."[80] The hijackers were sentenced to death on a Wednesday. Following established rules, the verdict was officially reviewed. The appeal was denied the next day, and that same evening the Council of State, the highest authority in such cases, convened in emergency session to confirm the verdict. Cubans learned on Friday morning from the news that the execution had already been carried out. Disagreement was widespread and pronounced. In light of the public reaction, Fidel Castro considered it necessary to appear on national television to explain the government's actions.[81] Tempers continued to run high in the wake of the arrests and executions, and criticism of the government was common.

In light of calls by the European Union and the United States to release the dissidents and mounting criticism of the death sentences, Cuban authorities defended the actions taken. In an April 2003 statement, Carlos Fernández de Cossio, the Cuban ambassador to Canada presented the Cuban government's view on the arrest and sentencing of the dissidents:

> The individuals arrested, prosecuted and sentenced in Cuba in recent days were not accused, nor were they detained, tried and sentenced for being economists, journalists, human rights activists or for expressing their opinion or dissent. They have violated laws clearly known by them that are aimed to legitimately protect Cuba from the attempt by the U.S. government to destabilize the country, undermine and destroy Cuba's constitutional order, its Government, its independence and its Socialist society. . . . It is illegal [in Cuba] to render to the U.S. government information that facilitates the implementation of the Helms-Burton law and other provisions of U.S. hostility toward Cuba. It is illegal to seek classified information to help the implementation of Helms-Burton. It is illegal to reproduce and distribute information materials of the U.S. government conceived to support the economic war against Cuba and disturb the internal order in the country. It is illegal to take actions in support of Helms-Burton that damage or obstruct the economic, industrial, commercial and financial relations of Cuban entities with the international community.
>
> The U.S. does not have the right in Cuba and should not have the right anywhere to instruct their diplomats to interfere in the domestic affairs of a foreign country. It is not acceptable to Cuba for the chief U.S. diplomat in Havana to act as an organizer or agitator against the Government and to have Cuban citizens acting not only in complicity but also as instruments of the policy of hostility of the U.S. against Cuba. The U.S. government has dedicated hundreds of millions of dollars and still dedicates millions of dollars today to destabilize the Cuban nation. It is a publicly documented fact. The actions for which these individuals have faced the law are organized, financed, and conceived by the U.S. government. Cuba has the right to defend itself against such powerful foe and protect the stability, security and the lives of its citizens. U.S. hostility against Cuba has cost already hundreds of lives, pain to many families, immense economic damage, and instability to the region. No

country that respects itself would allow its nation to face such dangers without protection. . . .

This is not an issue of human rights, liberty or freedom of expression; it is about the right of a nation to build a just society protected from foreign aggression. International Law is on Cuba's side. The government that has supported some of the most brutal regimes of the 20th century, that disregards international law, that steps over the UN, that carries out a criminal war for economic and geopolitical ambitions, that possesses the greatest arsenals of nuclear, chemical, and biological weapons cannot and should not be allowed to assume that Cuba's integrity and sovereignty are for sale (http://canadiannetworkoncuba.ca/documents/DeCossio—8apr03.shtml).

Whereas one might disagree with the reasoning presented here, one thing is irrefutable: the United States did indeed sponsor the activities of opposition groups. Ironically, it was exactly this U.S. backing that impeded the development of the Cuban opposition. U.S. policies have consistently undermined any genuine attempt to build an effective movement. Government officials have had an easy task in discrediting the dissidents. They could be credibly painted as puppets of the United States and, therefore, as illegitimate. Alarcón put it this way:

A person in Europe, in Austria, in the Philippines, in other parts [of the world], when one talks about the opposition, one has an idea that corresponds to the context. But in our case, what we are talking about is not the difference that could exist between a Social Democrat and Social Christian in Europe. We have a fabricated opposition. It is a unique case . . . it is the Cuba project. . . . According to General Kirkpatrick, the CIA inspector general, it began in the Spring of 1959. . . . The essence of the project consisted in creating an exile organization and, within Cuba, an opposition, nourished by strong external support. . . . Today you will find, under the same name, the Cuba Program. . . . The essence of the North American strategy in the handling of this conflict, from the beginning, was to hide its nature and present it as a problem between Cubans, that in Cuba there is some kind of civil war. . . . What used to be a covert operation in the 1960s, 1970s, [and] in the 1980s came to be a public policy with the passage of the Toricelli Law. Show me another law, in another country of the world, were another state arrogates to itself the capacity to create an opposition in another country. . . . In my judgment, it is unjust to make a comparison between the question of the opposition in Cuba and the opposition in any part of the world. To be in opposition is not an insult; many decent people oppose something at some point in their lives. But what we are talking about—which cannot be denied seriously—is something that corresponds to a deliberate plan by a foreign power with the objective to take possession of Cuba.

The majority of Cubans appear to hold similar views. As one Cuban, supportive of the revolution yet critical of many government policies, affirmed:

> I am a follower of Martí, and I really would prefer there to be a broader spectrum and that specific minority sectors would have the possibility of expressing themselves. However, the problem is that this opposition that exists in Cuba is not such an opposition. These people have no social base whatsoever. It is not going to be a minority with the mission to improve a project. . . . Up to this moment, I have not seen an opposition that is really a serious opposition, with a project. . . . What worries me is the political intention of the people that are active in this. Why are they doing it, what sectors do they represent, who supports them, what type of people are they? I won't be seduced by [beautiful] words. [On the other hand] I don't think that it is good that it is not being publicized.[82]

Cubans frequently express the view that they do not see the current opposition as legitimate, while at the same time they advocate greater freedom of expression for dissenting views. In the view of Max Azicri, a knowledgeable, longtime observer of the Cuban revolution, "putting pressure on Cuba to democratize the political system is counterproductive—especially if it comes from conservative Americans and Cuban Americans. Nothing could be less legitimate in Cuba than claims made by those that have been enemies of the revolution all along. The dissidents' major problem is the perception that they are Washington's tools and have been entrusted with the task of attacking the revolution from within."[83]

Conclusion: Competing Visions of Democracy

Any evaluation of the Cuban system of government solely from the perspective of liberal constitutionalism (i.e., traditional Western perspectives on democracy) leads to preordained conclusions. I concur with the growing number of scholars, politicians, and practitioners who have warned of the dangers of seeking to export and impose Western notions of democracy throughout the globe.[84] Afghanistan and Iraq are only the two most recent examples demonstrating the complexities involved in nation-building exercises. While I support the broader normative goals behind these exercises, the exercises themselves are fraught with problems. The overemphasis on formally competitive elections as an indicator of the establishment of democratic rule is particularly problematic. This reality entails lessons for current and future relations with Cuba.

While it is essential to criticize the Cuban government when human rights are threatened, Cuba deserves to be treated like any other country. The revolutionary government's record on human rights is deservedly criticized, and a host of human rights organizations have publicized serious violations of universally accepted human rights protocols.[85] Yet when Cuba is unjustly singled out by the United States and held to a different standard in obvious pursuit of a political agenda, such denunciations lack credibility and become counterproductive. Any meaningful analysis of the Cuban political system needs to employ a more inclusive framework, seeking to understand the Cuban system on its own terms.

The Cuban government has survived greater challenges to its authority over the long course of the revolution's history than the recent events depicted here. The spring 2003 challenge to the revolutionary government paled in comparison to the 1994 protests of almost a decade earlier. At that time thousands of Cubans openly protested at the Malecón, a famous seaside walkway in Havana. Leonardo Martínez recounted these events:

> [It was] the only time in [my] life that there was a demonstration here in Cuba of several thousands. [Fidel Castro] arrived and told his bodyguards: "No arms anyone. We are going there. Let them throw a stone, let them hit me." And he went into the middle of everybody in an open jeep, one of those Russian ones. And all those that were shouting, "Down with Fidel!" started [to shout], "Long live Fidel!"[86]

Many Cubans believe that Castro, who managed to defuse the 1994 crisis at the height of Cuba's economic difficulties, will easily outmaneuver these more recent challenges. Important developments support this view. In January 2005 the European Union suspended the "diplomatic freeze" it had imposed in response to the spring 2003 events. The reconsideration of the EU position came after more than a dozen prisoners had been released and several member countries, including Spain (led by Prime Minister José Luis Zapatero), had urged a review of EU policy toward Cuba.[87]

Ironically, the U.S. government continued to be Castro's greatest ally. Due to its actions, Cuban officials could argue that repressive measures were at times needed in defense of the country: "We must defend ourselves. We have the right and the duty to defend ourselves as a sovereign country, as a free, democratic country."[88] Furthermore, as long as the opposition is not considered authentic, it is easy to argue that it needs to be curtailed. Marta Harnecker emphasizes the unfair competition the Cuban government would face were it to open up its political system under the prevailing conditions:

> The problem is that if one permits [other] parties, one does not compete with the small groups that exist here. One starts to compete with the economic resources, with the propaganda that these people would bring. It would be like this: We can't invade Cuba, the Bay of Pigs [invasion] failed. It would be like giving them a beachhead so they could start to operate. . . . As long as this policy pursued by the United States exists, this revolution needs unity.[89]

Juan López, drawing on the regime transitions in Eastern Europe, has argued that two main factors explain the absence of transition in Cuba: (1) the majority of the Cuban people do not believe that change is possible (i.e., they lack a sense of political efficacy); and (2) there are not enough channels for independent sources of communication able to reach a large percentage of the population on a regular basis.[90] This is too simplistic a view of the Cuban context. López might be right in arguing that Cubans lack political efficacy, and independent media are definitely in short supply. The longevity of Castro's regime, however, cannot be explained exclusively by these factors. The fabric of Cuban society is far more complex. Under the current circumstances, most Cubans have either no desire to change the system or are convinced that they cannot afford to advocate change. There is still widespread loyalty and admiration for the current system, particularly among the generation that built the revolution. Equally important, and related to it: almost every Cuban has a personal stake in the system's survival. The revolution created a welfare state that protects the basic economic rights of every citizen. Cubans take the right to free education and health care for granted and expect the government to provide the most basic food items basically for free. Cubans generally live in apartments or houses that did not belong to them or their family before 1959. Thus, Cubans are afraid that they will be literally out on the streets if the current government falls and Cuban exiles return and claim their original properties.

Party and State

Gender Equality in Political Decision-making

[We have] a party in which there is a high percentage of men in the leadership, a government in which there is a very high percentage of men, so that it might seem to be a party of men and a government of men. The day must come when we have a party of men and women, and a leadership of men and women, and a state of men and women, and a government of men and women.

Fidel Castro

In 1966 Cuban leader Fidel Castro publicly recognized the importance of incorporating women fully into the new Cuban social project. At the time women were actively involved in changing the educational and health-care system and started to participate in the workforce in greater numbers. Their political participation as candidates and officeholders, however, proceeded more slowly. Castro recognized this in 1974 when he emphasized the lack of women's representation in party and state leadership structures and established gender equality as a goal. In his address (quoted above) to the Second Congress of the Cuban Federation of Women (FMC), the Cuban president described a gendered reality of the country's leadership structures that were dominated by men and expressed his conviction for the need to have women participate on a more equal footing.[1] The struggle for women's equality was a key issue debated at the First Congress of the Cuban Communist party held in 1975.[2] The basis for the discussion was a document entitled *Thesis: On the Full Exercise of Women's Equality*. It put the struggle for women's rights at the forefront of public discussion.

This chapter assesses the progress Cuba has made over the past thirty years on reaching the stated goal of establishing gender equality in decision-making. I explore the gender composition of Cuba's governmental structures, discuss efforts to strengthen women's political participation, and compare the inclusion of women into key state and party decision-making bodies. This chapter is guided by three main arguments. First, in Cuba's legislative structures women have a greater presence at the national than at the local level, contrary to the experience of the United States and Western Europe. Second, despite the official position denying the existence of gender quotas, Cuba does implement measures of positive discrimination in order to strengthen women's presence in politics. I argue that Cuban reality requires corrective measures in order to improve gender equality in decision-making and that there is evidence that measures of positive discrimination, albeit not in the form of official quotas, are operative. It is precisely this need for corrective action that appears to make Cuban officials so reluctant to acknowledge the existence of governmental initiatives to advance women in politics. In their mind, such an acknowledgment would imply a critique of the revolution itself.

Finally, Cuban women face a glass ceiling as they move up to positions of greater decision-making power, a reality faced by women all over the world. The excellent gender composition of Cuba's Parliament is an apparent exception that confirms the following rule: I assert that an examination of the state of gender equality in Cuba's decision-making structures reveals an inverse relationship between the actual decision-making power of a particular institution and the presence of women. That is, the higher we get in the institutional decision-making hierarchy, the fewer women we find. Evidence for these arguments can be found by analyzing the gender composition of state and party structures.

The Gender Composition of People's Power

Three patterns characterize women's participation in Cuba's people's power assemblies: (1) the difference in the gender composition at the local versus the national level; (2) the noticeable decline in female representation in the early 1990s; and (3) the high number of women in the National Assembly. According to the Inter-Parliamentary Union (IPU), in February 2006 only six countries had a higher percentage of women in their parliaments.[3]

As noted in table 4.1, women's participation in the National Assembly reached an initial high point in 1986, when 34 percent of the deputies were women. This was a substantial increase from the level of 23 percent female representation in 1981. By 1993, however, the number of women deputies was back to the level of the early 1980s. That year, 134 women (22.8 percent) were elected to the Cuban Parliament, composed of 589 members. Five years later, women's representation had increased to 28 percent. As a result of the 2003 elections, the legislature increased its share of female deputies dramatically. It had 219 women (36 percent) out of a total of 609 members. About half (53 percent) of the female delegates were white, with the rest being black or mestizo.

As table 4.1 shows, the gender composition of the provincial assemblies was relatively similar to the one observed in the case of the Parliament. Over the

Table 4.1. Women's Participation in Cuba's Poder Popular, 1976–2003

Level of Decision-making	Number and Percentage of Women											
	1976		1981		1986		1993		1998		2003	
National Assembly	105	21.8	113	22.7	173	33.9	134	22.8	166	27.6	219	35.9
Provincial Assemblies	192	17.2	191	16.8	426	30.8	284	23.9	342	28.6	451	37.6
Municipal Assemblies	856	8.2	837	7.8	2,264	17.1	1,879	13.5	2,595	17.9	3,493	23.4

Source: Comisión Electoral Nacional

past decade, women fared slightly better in the provinces. At the municipal level, however, far fewer women tended to participate. In 1981 women represented less than 8 percent of all municipal delegates. The gender composition of the local assemblies became somewhat more equal over the years. By the late 1990s it reached 18 percent, and following the 2002–2003 elections, women made up 23 percent of the assemblies.

At all levels, we observe a decline in women's representation in the early 1990s. This precipitous reduction was related to the economic crisis that ensued in the wake of the demise of the Soviet Union and Cuba's Eastern European allies. The loss of its major trading partners had serious repercussions for the country and led to a deterioration in the already difficult situation for women. It complicated women's daily lives and made them reluctant to assume the burden of public office. It is generally recognized that due to "the scarcity of consumer goods and other hardships in the 1990s, women had to concentrate their efforts on the home front."[4] Mayda Álvarez, an FMC leader and researcher, has argued that the decline in female representation in the early 1990s can be attributed to subjective and objective factors: the objective factors included women's workload in the home, particularly the responsibility of caring for children and the lack of material resources.[5] The subjective factors, on the other hand, were rooted in men's unwillingness to nominate women as candidates. Men's decisions were often based on stereotypes and prejudice: "The fear that women can't do a good job because of lack of time"; "women have children or will have them"; "not being accustomed to be led by women"; or "considering that women are less efficient than men."[6]

In contrast to the experience of most countries, women's representation was considerably lower at the municipal level than at the national level. The smallest difference was a gap of 9 points in 1993. It reached a high of almost 17 points in 1986. Following the last election, there remained a substantial gap of 12.5 points. Thus, the much lower representation of women at the local level is noticeable and demands an explanation. At the local level, women face substantial hurdles in getting elected. As table 4.2 demonstrates, their challenges start in being chosen as candidates.

Table 4.2. Gender Composition of Candidates to the Municipal Assemblies, 1976–2005

Mandate	Women	%	Men	%	Total
1976–79	3,946	13.5	25,223	86.5	29,169
1979–81	2,402	9.9	21,859	90.1	24,261
1981–84	2,693	11.4	20,974	88.6	23,667
1984–86	3,769	16.3	19,349	83.7	23,118
1986–89	6,191	22.2	21,644	77.8	27,835
1989–92	5,816	19.7	23,689	80.3	29,505
1992–95	4,226	14.8	24,248	85.2	28,474
1995–97	4,656	14.6	24,313	85.4	28,969
1997–2000	5,785	18.4	25,491	81.6	31,276
2000–2003	6,640	21.4	24,363	78.6	31,003
2003–2006	—	—	—	—	36,955

Source: Calculated based on data in Iraida Aguirrechu and José Quesada, *Poder Popular*, annex; National Election Commission

In the first elections in 1976, 13.5 percent of the candidates to the municipal assemblies were women. Of the 3,946 women that were nominated, only 856 (21 percent) were elected. Men had a much higher success rate. Of the 25,223 male candidates, 9,869 (39 percent) became members of the municipal assemblies. Thus, men were almost twice as successful in getting elected. In the next election cycle in 1979, there were even fewer female candidates (less than 10 percent). Although a somewhat higher percentage of them (32 percent) got elected, female representation in the municipal assemblies that year was only 7 percent.

The number of female candidates rose in subsequent years, both in absolute terms and in terms of gender distribution. A decade later, female candidates represented about 20 percent of all candidates. However, in the 1992 and 1995 elections, when Cuba suffered its worst economic crisis since the beginning of the revolution, the data show a significant drop in female candidates to less than 15 percent. At the same time, however, those women who were nominated had a much better chance of getting elected than their cohorts of the previous decades. In 1976, 13.5 percent of those nominated were women, as were 8 percent of the elected delegates. By 1995, however, 14.6 percent of those nominated were women, while 15.5 percent of those elected were female. Thus, once women agreed to run, they had the same chance as their male counterparts of getting elected. Table 4.3 presents the gender composition of the local assemblies. Women's representation started at a very low level (less than 10 percent) and became more equal over time.

In the 2002 elections, women's representation reached 23 percent. Although this was a considerable improvement compared with earlier elections, female

Table 4.3. Gender Composition of the Municipal Assemblies, 1976–2005

Mandate	Women	%	Men	%	Total
1976–79	856	8.0	9,869	92.0	10,725
1979–81	764	7.2	9,892	92.8	10,656
1981–84	837	7.8	9,898	92.2	10,735
1984–86	1,261	11.5	9,702	88.5	10,963
1986–89	2,264	17.1	10,992	82.9	13,256
1989–92	2,378	16.6	11,868	83.4	14,246
1992–95	1,879	13.6	11,986	86.4	13,865
1995–97	2,211	15.5	12,018	84.5	14,229
1997–2000	2,595	17.8	11,938	82.2	14,533
2000–2003	3,081	20.9	11,605	79.1	14,686
2003–2006	3,493	23.4	11,453	76.6	14,946

Source: Calculated based on data in Iraida Aguirrechu and José Quesada, *Poder Popular*, annex; National Election Commission

Table 4.4. Gender Composition of the Provincial Assemblies, 1976–2008

Mandate	Women	%	Men	%	Total
1976–79	192	17.2	923	82.8	1,115
1979–81	198	17.4	941	82.6	1,139
1981–84	191	16.8	948	83.2	1,139
1984–86	294	21.4	1,083	78.6	1,377
1986–89	426	30.8	962	69.2	1,388
1989–93	390	27.6	1,023	72.4	1,413
1993–98	284	23.8	906	76.2	1,190
1998–2003	342	28.7	850	71.3	1,192
2003–2008	451	37.6	748	62.4	1,199

Source: Calculated based on data in Iraida Aguirrechu and José Quesada, *Poder Popular*, annex; National Election Commission
Note: In the 1976–89 elections, the municipal assemblies elected the delegates to the provincial assemblies for a period of two and a half years. Following the 1992 constitutional reform, the voting system was changed to direct elections and the mandate was extended to five years.

representation at the local level continued to be substantially below that of the provincial and national level. The leadership of the local assemblies was also largely male. Only 19 women (11 percent) served as president of one of the 169 municipal councils. About 25 percent of the vice presidents were female, and as traditional gender relations would lead us to expect, women held almost 50 percent of the municipal secretary positions.[7] In the provinces, female representation was consistently a significant 10 percent higher than at the local level.

In 1976 women represented 17 percent of the provincial delegates. Over

Table 4.5. Gender Composition of the National Assembly, 1976–2008

Legislative Period	Women	%	Men	%	Total
1976–81	105	21.8	376	78.2	481
1981–86	113	22.6	386	77.4	499
1986–93	173	33.9	337	66.1	510
1993–98	134	22.7	455	77.3	589
1998–2003	166	27.6	435	72.4	601
2003–2008	219	35.9	390	64.1	609

Source: Calculated based on data in Iraida Aguirrechu and José Quesada, *Poder Popular*, annex; National Election Commission
Note: In the 1976–86 elections, the municipal assemblies elected the delegates to the National Assembly. Following the 1992 constitutional reform, the voting system was changed to direct elections.

the years, women's representation increased and reached over 30 percent at the time of the 1986 elections. This improvement was followed by the already discussed decline of the mid-1990s. In the 2003 elections, however, there was a considerable increase in women legislators to almost 38 percent, surpassing even the National Assembly's gender balance.

At the leadership level, however, women were hardly to be found. Not a single woman served as president of a provincial assembly following the 2002–2003 election. About 21 percent of the vice presidents were women, and repeating the pattern from the local level, women held almost 43 percent of all secretary positions.[8]

In the National Assembly, women started with almost 22 percent representation in 1976. Over the next two decades, the gender composition of the National Assembly followed the established pattern, with a substantial increase in the mid-1980s to 34 percent and a subsequent decline. Although the country's record was respectable by international standards, the gender composition of the Cuban Parliament before the 2003 elections was considered unsatisfactory. Leonardo Martínez, who headed the National Assembly's powerful Standing Committee for Productive Activities, affirmed:

> We all are greatly dissatisfied in Cuba. What happens: more than 60 percent of all middle- and high-level professionals in Cuba are women. Thus, women should be represented more or less in this proportion. Higher than what we have. . . . I consider 27 percent [before 2003] not bad. For Latin America this is not bad. But when you compare this with other parliaments and with the strength that women have in Cuban society, women should be without doubt better represented.[9]

The 2003 elections resulted in the most equal parliamentary gender composition in Cuba's history. It put Cuba into a select group of countries that could claim more that 30 percent female representation in their parliaments.

As the data presented above demonstrate, the difference in representation levels between the national and local levels was pronounced and remained relatively constant over time. Women's representation in Parliament was consistently 10 percent higher than at the local level. Yet based on the "pipeline theory" developed in the U.S. context, we would expect to find the highest level of female representation at the local level. As Georgia Duerst-Lahti has argued, "experience in one elected office is seen as providing credentials for other offices."[10] As we will see, the Cuban anomaly—having more female representatives at the national level than at the local level—is easily explained, once we take the decision-making power of the respective bodies into account.

Explaining the Cuban Anomaly

I would argue that the differences in the gender composition of the national versus the local legislative bodies have their roots in three key realities: (1) the work burden and time commitment entailed in serving on a municipal assembly versus the Parliament; (2) a *machista* culture that has greater impact at the local level due to electoral rules; and (3) the conscious efforts by officials to change the gender composition of decision-making structures at the national level.

Eduardo Freire, president of the National Candidate Commission, emphasized the heavy workload carried by municipal assembly delegates:

> Everything that originates at the level of the nation and in the province is executed in the township. That's where the hole in the road is, where the gas tank is missing, where the potatoes didn't arrive, or the liter of milk was cut. This is the situation at the grassroots [level]. [The problems exist] every day and constantly. You come home from work, tired and exhausted and . . . "There is no electricity!" That is it. One must have a special capacity for service to the *patria* (nation) in order to fulfill this duty, and many *compañeros* and *compañeras* do it with great dignity and with a lot of integrity. But these are the moments that we are living.[11]

Therefore, serving on a municipal assembly requires a considerable amount of idealism, particularly in light of the fact that members are not paid for their work, which is time-consuming and demanding. Due to the workload at the municipal level, women are reluctant to take on duties as a delegate. Ricardo

Alarcón, president of the National Assembly, summarized women's senti-ments: "I have a house to keep, I have to cook, I have to go shopping . . . and at times there is no water, the electricity goes out; all these problems are associ-ated with the woman, not the man. They are not shared."[12] Frequently, women who have served in office are not eager to seek reelection. On the contrary, "I have seen female delegates coaxing the [neighborhood] assembly so they elect someone else, not her, and she explains: 'I have two children. . . . I don't want to get involved in this.'"[13] At the time of nominating candidates, local voters who do not want to impose additional burdens on a woman recognize these challenging circumstances. In light of them, women and men tend to prefer male candidates, particularly when "there is a *señor* with a beginning belly who has time on his hands and is disposed to collaborate."[14]

The time commitment for a member of the National Assembly, on the other hand, is quite limited. Parliament meets only twice a year for a few days. As in the case of the local level, national delegates receive no additional com-pensation for their work. Instead, they continue to be paid a regular salary from their original workplace. Thus, the key difference between the local and the national bodies is that serving on a municipal assembly is considerably more demanding than being a member of Parliament. In the eyes of many observers, until Alarcón assumed the leadership of the National Assembly in the 1990s, the Cuban Parliament was considered an overly formalistic body "which functioned more as a meeting of celebrities than as a forum of legisla-tors who have to be accountable to the voters."[15] Indeed, the 2003 National As-sembly included sports stars; prominent writers and such famous musicians as songwriter Silvio Rodríguez; Ana Fidelia Quirot, a world champion over 800 meters; as well as high jumper Alberto Juantorena. Juan Miguel González, a waiter who gained international prominence due to his custody battle with the U.S. government over his son Elián, joined other personalities of national reputation in Parliament. Since the cost of serving in Parliament was not that high and more glamorous, it is not surprising that it is easier to find women candidates willing to run for national office than for a town council.

The second point concerning differences in female representation at the national versus the local level is rooted in the Cuban culture of *machismo*. Mayda Álvarez and her colleagues put it this way:

The fact that the participation of women in People's Power is higher at the national level and lower at the grassroots level . . . has its origin in the perception that our society still maintains about [the image of] the leader. When positions are determined by direct vote, there are more possibilities that beliefs, prejudices, and cultural patterns inherited from a class-based and sexist society are expressed, which assign to the man the world of work and public power and to the woman the realm of the home; that is to say, the social perception still assigns a preferential masculine face to leadership.[16]

Álvarez's explanation was partially based on the old voting system under which only delegates to the local level of government were elected by direct vote. Although legislators at all levels have been chosen in direct elections since 1992, the potential impact of the direct vote was controlled in the case of the National Assembly due to the fact that there was only one candidate for every seat in Parliament. Thus, the gender of a particular candidate could not be a factor in the voter's choice. While voters could refrain from voting for a specific candidate, they could not express a preference for male over female candidates or vice versa.

Therefore, women candidates at the local level are to a greater degree subject to the dominant gender relations informed by traditional views on leadership than their counterparts at the national level. Jesús García, a former delegate and author of a study on Cuba's system of government called *Poder Popular*, affirmed this:

We can control the composition of the provincial assembly and of the national assembly better than the composition of the town councils. This means that in the case of the provincial and the national assemblies there is a candidate list elaborated by the Candidate Commission. For the municipal councils, nominations are totally free and totally uncontrollable and come from the population. Thus, it is the general public that continues to hold prejudices. Not so much prejudices but realities. The Cuban woman still carries the household responsibilities that people consider as limiting at times in completing other activities. It is for this reason that the people in the neighborhoods limit themselves at times in nominating women.[17]

Women themselves were captives of the *machista* culture. Freire shared his experience of observing the deliberation of women members of the commission that selects candidates:

What operates here, at times, is the false machismo of the *compañeras*. Among each other they say: "Poor Aidita, who has two little kids, for what reason are we going to involve her in this responsibility." It also has something to do with how we Cubans are, with this sense of protection toward a woman so she can fulfill her duty in the family. We men also have it, but, well, the sentiments from the past remain. However, this is changing, and when these things happen it is between ourselves. At times we see ourselves saying: "We will not include Aidita who has three small children." And perhaps we have not consulted her. Maybe you ask her [and she responds]: "It doesn't matter to me. I have three kids but I am [willing to be a candidate for] delegate or deputy."[18]

Whereas some women are reluctant to serve, others are victims of a *machista* culture. Despite significant cultural change over the course of the Cuban revolution, machismo has nonetheless been a constant in Cuban political culture. As a result, the most important factor explaining the difference in representation levels can be found in the authorities' ability to control the gender composition of the National Assembly.

Cuban Efforts to Strengthen Women's Political Participation

Mala Htun has reported that "some 50 countries officially allocate access to political power along the lines of gender, ethnicity, or both: they have laws on the books reserving a fixed number of electoral candidacies or legislative seats."[19] Htun emphasizes that institutional remedies differ for women and ethnic groups. Whereas women are generally allocated candidate quotas in political parties, the remedy for underrepresentation in the case of ethnic minorities tends to consist of having seats reserved in the legislature.[20] In Latin America, twelve countries have adopted gender quotas since 1990, with Cuba not being part of this group.

Htun presents evidence indicating that "military governments, one-party states, no-party states, and other countries that fail to respect civil liberties" are more likely to give women reserved seats instead of candidate quotas. She argues convincingly that "granting reserved seats to women allows nondemocracies to respond to popular pressure and conform to international norms without ceding ground to the competitive party politics presumed by candidate quotas. Yet the very nature of such regimes prevents female—and male—legislators from representing citizen interests and wielding effective power."[21] Thus, the reservation of seats tends to have a demobilizing effect, whereas quotas on party lists tend to stimulate societal discourse on the merits of gender equality.

Cuba, a one-party state, has no official gender quotas. There is clear evidence, however, that measures of positive discrimination have been instituted. I argue that the Cuban system is de facto closer to a reservation of seats than a system of candidate quotas, a reality that has a negative societal impact. It preempts coalition building for greater gender equality.

Officially, Cuban authorities have argued against the use of quotas or other measures of positive discrimination designed to increase women's participation in decision-making. Roberto Díaz, the minister of justice, strongly denied the existence of quotas: "Here [in Cuba], we don't have a quota. No, no, no. The voters get together in the candidate nomination areas, and [they choose among candidates] according to their merits, their background, [and] their capacity to serve the people."[22] When asked to explain the difference in female representation at the local versus the national level, Díaz offered this explanation for the lower female participation rate in the municipal assemblies: "I think that spontaneity operates here to a great degree. That is to say, it is not a directed affair. It [a corrective mechanism] does not exist because I can tell you that the majority [of the candidates] are party militants, and the party militants are not being controlled."[23] Thus, Díaz is representative of Cuban officials who feel obliged to deny that the government implements quotas but implicitly acknowledge the existence of measures to increase gender equality at the national level when discussing the electoral process.

National Assembly president Alarcón affirmed that quotas were frowned upon, presumably because they are seen as measures that are favored by "Western interests." While Alarcón did "not think that it would be correct to establish a quota system as it is done in some countries,"[24] he was not in principle against measures of positive discrimination. For example, Alarcón argued that it was in his power to see to it that women obtained representation in the Cuban Parliament's working commissions:

> This is something that the Americans call "affirmative action," that is, actions one can take. What one cannot do is to invent or to change what the people are going to do when they vote their conscience. . . . The problem would be if we were to be ultrademocratic. Because if we were to do exactly what the people want . . . the situation of women would not improve. Thus, we need to force it, force the hand a tiny little bit, a little bit, with certain limits because you can't impose it fully.[25]

This amazing statement reveals not only that various manifestations of affirmative action are a part of Cuban reality but that Cuban political leaders perceive a need to intervene in order to establish gender equality in the political arena. Despite Alarcón's recognition of the predominance of traditional gender relations that discriminate against women and his acknowledgment that he had the prerogative to strengthen women's participation in these important commissions, little was being done to give more women access to these leadership positions. Whereas the main business of the Parliament was conducted by its ten permanent commissions, women were given traditional roles. With the exception of two commissions—Defense and Foreign Relations—all had a female secretary. On the other hand, only two had a female president.[26]

Affirmative action in various manifestations is obviously a part of Cuban life. María Josefa Ruíz, one of the women serving in the National Assembly, emphasized that the candidate selection process at the national level had a gender component and pointed out the benefits of diversity:

> People [should] understand that we must be together [in the fight to end discrimination]. When there is a woman and a man with identical qualifications, we will choose the woman. . . . We choose the woman and [therefore] have greater representativeness . . . greater balance. When there is a black and a white [candidate] with the same qualifications, we will pick the black person. The legislative body does not lose, and [it] attains a composition where increasingly we are all represented. This type [of positive discrimination] is being done.[27]

The Cuban authorities work to consciously address gender imbalances. In fact, the leadership has recognized prevailing gender inequities in numerous speeches and documents, and a long-standing campaign has sought to address them. Fidel Castro, together with other high-ranking officials, has consistently advocated greater gender equality.

Some women leaders acknowledge that quotas were useful tools in the early struggle to increase women's participation. Mavis Álvarez, a key figure in the struggle to strengthen women's leadership in the rural sector, acknowledged the existence of quotas:

> There are no quotas [now]. But there was a time when they did exist, when one had to establish quotas. Otherwise there would be no women. There was a time when you had to tell them [the male leaders] in effect: "Listen! At least 5 percent or 10 percent must be women." But it was also a policy of the party to establish quotas. Because without pressure there would be none [i.e., women being elected]. However, this is no longer the case. It is no longer necessary to do this because of an increase in consciousness so that every time a body of leaders is elected, it is always thought that women must be part of it.[28]

Reportedly, Fidel Castro himself considered the necessity of quotas. Nieves Alemañy, a member of the FMC's national leadership, recounted exchanges between the Women's Federation and Castro:

> *El Jefe* [the boss], who knows that quotas exist in other countries, . . . consulted with the federation [to see] whether we considered it neces-

sary to establish quotas in order to promote women's development and women's participation. We told him no, that with the conditions prevailing in Cuba it appeared to us that it would not be necessary. Little by little, women would reach the necessary levels from a cultural, technical, and professional point of view and would acquire the training necessary for leadership.[29]

Thus, the FMC itself argued against the introduction of official quotas at the same time that many of the organization's leaders expressed concern in FMC meetings and publications about the scarcity of women in positions of leadership. Behind this official façade, however, significant measures were taken to improve the gender composition of some governmental bodies, albeit not the most significant ones.

By far the most effective effort to achieve greater gender equality was located in the work of the National Candidate Commission. The high level of women's representation in Cuba's Parliament is a direct result of the commission's policies. While acknowledging their efforts to improve the gender balance of national and provincial candidate lists, commission officials were adamant that there was no quota system. They insisted that female candidates were selected purely based on merit. Eduardo Freire, the commission's president, emphasized this point in the months leading up to the 2002-03 elections:

Well, the first thing I would like to tell you is that there is no quota. It is not because of a quota, not because of an [established] norm [that women are included]. We are going to evaluate merit, we are going to evaluate capacity, we are going to evaluate disposition, and the women only emerge based on this evaluation. This process will always require an adjustment from the point of view of composition and representativeness that we talked to you about. For example, if we are going to form a National Assembly, not all [candidates] can be women nor can all of them be men. But there is no intentionality anywhere to say: "Here we need ten more women to get to the 30 percent. Or here we need to put five more women." No, no, no! We make an evaluation of what [the candidate pool] gives. And what it gives it gives. If what it gives is 15 percent [female representation], this does not correspond with the development women have had in the country. This is a hypothetical example that I'm telling you. It didn't come out this way. And I can tell you that in the first approximation that we have of the [candidate] projects we are making, the number of women that have emerged is tremendous. ... That today there will be a lot more [women] than are currently there [in the National Assembly] is a result of this recognition that they have gained due to their work.[30]

Roberto Díaz basically affirmed Freire's account, acknowledging that gender is a factor in the selection process:

The only thing that the Candidate Commission does is to make a nomination, but the Candidate Commission does not make decisions. The Candidate Commission can make a nomination that comes precisely from the base organizations. . . . Well, it could be that the Candidate Commission says, "I have here nominations from the Cuban Women's Federation. I don't know—twenty men and twenty women. I will take ten of each. I'm going to establish a candidate list." [or] "I'll take fifteen women and five men." It can do it. But it is not that the element of the [candidate's] sex is given preference, it is an ingredient, but it is not the only one.[31]

Thus, while government officials object to quotas, they acknowledge that the CNC takes gender into consideration in creating the candidate lists. Actually, the corrective measures implemented by the CNC have been quite comprehensive and are the key explanation for the relatively high levels of female representation at the national level. For example, in order to get from 18 percent female representation in the municipalities in 1997 to 28 percent at the national level, the National Candidate Commission had to make female candidates a top priority. Leonardo Martínez, a key figure in the National Assembly, explicitly affirmed this: we "privilege" female candidates.[32] Martínez was referring to the fact that according to Cuban election law, up to 50 percent of the candidates for the National Assembly are drawn from the pool of elected municipal assembly delegates. The other 50 percent are "national interest candidates."

Let us examine the process of "privileging" women in the 2002–2003 elections. The pool of municipal assembly members elected in fall 2002 who were potential candidates for Parliament had a relatively low number of women— 23.4 percent. Since all elected municipal assembly delegates, regardless of their sex, had distinguished records, one would expect that women and men would have similar success rates in getting chosen as candidates for a seat in Parliament. This was not the case, however. The outcome of the candidate selection process clearly indicates that the Candidate Commission gave preferential treatment to women.

Table 4.6 illustrates this important point. In the 2003 parliamentary elections, 609 candidates emerged out of the complex nomination process directed by the National Candidate Commission. Of this total, 283 candidates

Table 4.6. Gender Composition of National Assembly Candidates Drawn from Municipal Assemblies by Province, 2003

Province	Women Total	%	Men Total	%	Total
Pinar del Río	8	42.1	11	57.9	19
La Habana	13	65.0	7	35.0	20
Ciudad de la Habana	23	44.2	29	55.8	52
Matanzas	10	55.6	8	44.4	18
Isla de la Juventud	1	50.0	1	50.0	2
Villa Clara	11	55.0	9	45.0	20
Cienfuegos	4	36.4	7	63.6	11
Sancti Spíritus	6	54.6	5	45.4	11
Ciego de Ávila	7	58.3	5	41.7	12
Camagüey	12	57.1	9	42.9	21
Las Tunas	6	50.0	6	50.0	12
Holguín	12	50.0	12	50.0	24
Granma	5	26.3	14	73.7	19
Santiago de Cuba	10	40.0	15	60.0	25
Guantánamo	7	43.8	6	56.2	16
Total	135	47.70	148	52.3	283

Source: Álvarez, "Poder sin quotas," 19

(46.5 percent) had originally been elected to a municipal assembly. The gender composition of these "grassroots" candidates to Parliament was very balanced. There were 135 female and 148 male nominees, selected from a pool of 3,493 female and 11,453 male municipal delegates. Thus, whereas 3.86 percent of all female delegates were selected, only 1.3 percent of their male colleagues were successful. This means that female municipal assembly candidates were *almost three times* as successful as their male counterparts in getting selected for the candidate lists to the National Assembly. The only reasonable explanation for this is the preference given to women by the National Candidate Commission.

There was considerable variation across the provinces in the gender composition of the candidates that were chosen. The vanguard was the city of Havana, where 65 percent of the municipal candidates selected for inclusion on the parliamentary candidate list were female. Eight out of fifteen provinces achieved at least gender equity in their nominee distribution. Only Granma Province was an outlier, with 26 percent female representation.

It is intriguing that the remaining half of the candidates for Parliament—who are chosen based on their national stature in government, the Communist party, culture, and sports—exhibited a more unequal gender composition. The 326 national candidates consisted of 84 women (less than 26 percent) and

326 men. This confirms that the commission privileged female municipal delegates, but when it came to the selection of figures of national stature, women were not given preference. This appears to confirm that women have a difficult time rising to national prominence and that members of the commission have clear limits in how far they are permitted and/or willing to go in applying measures of affirmative action.

In summary, it is in the Candidate Commission where gender imbalances are addressed. Although the commission's proposals needed to be confirmed by the municipal assemblies, approval of the lists was routine. Whereas the work of the commission has generated high numbers of women in elective office at the national level, this unique Cuban approach to the achievement of gender equality has serious negative implications for society as a whole. Most importantly, the Cuban system has given government officials the right to determine when and where the gender composition of a particular decision-making body needs to be adjusted. Significantly, similar measures have not been taken in the most important structures of the Communist party, where real power is located.

The Scarcity of Women in Top Party and State Structures

The closer one moves to the pinnacles of real power, the fewer women one finds. The data clearly demonstrate that there is an inverse relationship between the power of a particular institution and its gender composition. In the Council of State, a key decision-making body that acts on behalf of the Parliament when the assembly is not in session, women's representation was about half of that in the National Assembly. In order to get a seat on the council, a candidate had to be nominated by the National Candidate Commission. The commission composed its list from the members of the National Assembly, seeking to include the most important ministers, the heads of the mass organizations, as well as representatives from other important state institutions. Freire, the head of the commission, insisted that in cases where the commission has the option of choosing between a woman and a man with equal merits, "we choose the woman."[33] Assuming this is indeed the case, the low level of female representation reflects the fact that few women have risen through the system acquiring the credentials considered necessary—by the male leadership—to occupy key positions of power.

Since 1993 the Council of State has been composed of thirty-one members. Five women have served in the council during the last decade, leaving female representation at 16 percent. In 2003 six women were elected, representing close to 20 percent of the council members. This figure was quite respectable

Table 4.7. Gender Composition of Cuba's Council of State, 1991–2003

Year	Women	%	Men	%
1991	4	13.8	25	86.2
1993	5	16.1	26	83.9
1998	5	16.1	26	83.9
2003	6	19.4	25	80.6

Source: Data for 1991 and 1993 based on data in Rodríguez Calderón, *Queda mucho por andar*, n.d.; data for 1998 based on Azicri, *Cuba Today and Tomorrow*, 309–12; date for 2003 based on *Granma*, March 7, 2003.

by international standards but did not reflect the favorable gender balance of the Parliament, which served as the council's recruiting pool. In terms of ministerial portfolios held by women, Cuba ranked thirty-fifth in the world as of January 2005. There were six women (16.2 percent) among the thirty-seven government ministers.[34]

Many Cuban officials argue that women's representation in government structures needed improvement. Alarcón put it quite bluntly: "It is evident that it is still very insufficient. Suffice it to contrast the role women play in Cuban society, in culture, in education, in science, in research, including in [the sphere of] production, with the one they have in politics."[35] Whereas female representation in the Council of State could be improved, the real problem is located elsewhere.

To reiterate, Cuba is a one-party state, and all key decisions are made in the two main party structures, both headed by Fidel Castro: the Politburo and the Central Committee. As in all other areas of life, the party is the hegemonic force in the realm of gender relations as well. Therefore, it is particularly relevant to examine the party's gender composition.

The data on the gender composition of the Cuban Communist party demonstrate that women's representation has increased over time. In the early years of the revolution, women were a distinct minority among the party members. For example, in 1967 women constituted only 10 percent of the membership. Their numbers grew to 15 percent by 1974.[36] From 1985 to 1993, female membership increased at a steady pace from less than 22 percent to 26 percent.[37] At the time of the last party congress in 1997, women represented about 30 percent of the 780,000 party militants.[38]

Carollee Bengelsdorf has argued that the unequal gender composition of the party is rooted in Cuba's sexual division of labor. Indeed, the regular way to party membership is through one's workplace. Although women are well represented in the labor force, their unequal burden in terms of work and domestic responsibilities makes it less likely that they will distinguish them-

Table 4.8. Women's Participation in the Cuban Communist Party (PCC), 1993–1997

Membership Level	Percent Women 1993	Percent Women 1997	Percent Change 1993–97	Rate of Increase
Provincial Committee	20.6	23.0	2.4	11.7
Municipal Committee	15.5[a]	22.0	6.5	41.9
Party Professionals	19.5	25.0	5.5	28.2
Party Members	26.3	30.1	3.8	14.4
Average	20.5	25.0	4.5	24.1

Source: PCC–Departamento de Organización
Note: (a) The reliability of the 1993 figure is in question. Official data from the Central Committee of the PCC, cited in Rodríguez Calderón (n.d., 30), report 25.5 percent for 1993, whereas PCC data in several archives indicate 15.5 percent. I use the latter figure instead of the one reported in Rodríguez Calderón, since it appears consistent with low levels of participation in other party and mass organization structures in the wake of Cuba's economic crisis of the early 1990s.

selves at work, a prerequisite for being invited into the party.[39] In 1997 about 30 percent of the party membership consisted of exemplary workers who had been recommended for party membership by their respective work centers.[40] In this context, it is interesting to note that for nearly thirty years, housewives were excluded from party membership.[41]

Although female membership in local and regional leadership structures does not correspond to women's strength among the party membership, the differences are relatively small. For example, in municipal committees we observe levels of representation around 20 percent, with the exception of 1993, when a low point of 15.5 percent was reached. On the other hand, female participation in the provincial committees reached a high in 1988, when women represented 24.5 percent. Their numbers decreased to a little over 20 percent in 1993. In 1997 the gender distribution in the provincial committees showed 23 percent women. Since women represented 29 percent of the 767,944 party militants in 1996,[42] women should have held about 6 percent more of the committee seats, which is not very significant.

Thus, as table 4.8 shows, the average percentage of women across the various levels of the party rose 5 percentage points, from 20.5 percent in 1993 to 25 percent by 1997. The average rate of increase for women at the various levels of party organization was 24 percent, the most significant improvement occurring at the municipal level.

The problem, as always, could be found in the top regional party ranks. For example, following the 1997 party congress, only two women (13 percent) held

Table 4.9. Gender Composition of the PCC's Leadership Structures, 1985–1997

Year	Politburo				Central Committee			
	Women	%	Men	%	Women	%	Men	%
1985	3	11.5	23	88.5	41	18.2	184	81.8
1991	3	11.5	23	88.5	38	16.9	187	83.1
1997	2	8.3	22	91.7	20	13.3	130	86.7

Source: Data for 1985–91 calculated by author based on data in Rodríguez Calderón, *Queda mucho por andar*, n.d.; data for 1997 based on Azicri, *Cuba Today and Tomorrow*, 311–12, and Randall, *Gathering Rage*, 152; *Granma*, Oct. 11, 1997

a position of first secretary on any of the party's fifteen provincial committees, including the Isle of Youth.[43] One of them was Yadira García, also a member of the Politburo, who served in the province of Matanzas, a key tourist area. María del Carmen Concepción held the only other position of first secretary in Pinar del Río.

The situation at the national level is similar. It is extremely difficult for female leaders to gain entry into the exclusive ranks of the inner sanctum of power, the Politburo and the Central Committee. For a long time, Vilma Espín, the head of the Cuban Women's Federation and one-time spouse of Raúl Castro, was the only woman who held full membership on the Politburo.[44]

Following elections in 1985 and 1991, three women were incorporated into the Politburo, representing 11.5 percent of the twenty-six members. Yet at the Fifth Party Congress in 1997, only two women were elected to the twenty-four-member Politburo. One of them was Yadira García, the Matanzas party official, with Concepción Campa holding the other seat. Campa is a renowned scientist who headed the successful effort to develop a new meningitis vaccine and served as the director of the Finlay Institute. The institute is key to the country's effort to strengthen its competitiveness in biomedical research. Cuba is a main supplier of vaccine to Latin America and is investing heavily in biomedical research.

Women did only slightly better at the level of the Central Committee. In this important decision-making body, female representation decreased from 18 percent in 1985 to 17 percent in 1991. In that year, 38 women were elected to the Central Committee, consisting of 225 members.[45] In 1997 the Central Committee was reduced to 150 members. According to official data, only twenty members (13 percent) were women.[46]

There is no single explanation for the scarcity of women in higher party ranks. Cultural factors, combined with practical and institutional impediments, have led to this outcome. According to National Assembly member María Josefa Ruíz:

Our party has the leadership role. . . . thus we are talking about decision-making, important decisions. Well, many women are there. But in the end it seems to us that fundamentally it has to be men who must take the main responsibilities. If we analyze the leadership of the party at its different levels, we'll see that the main leader is male and many women occupy second positions. . . . I think that women still have a lot of ground to gain, and this has to do with a world that used to be a masculine world, where the woman had the role to help the men live, to enjoy themselves, to rest, so they could continue to lead. Well, we have broken down the walls of the home, but look what we are still missing, we are missing a lot.[47]

Women in the party hierarchy reach a glass ceiling as they rise through the ranks. Although they have significant representation in leadership positions at the local and regional levels, they are not as readily accepted into high party positions as their male counterparts. The data supported two main conclusions: (1) few women were permitted into the corridors of power; and (2) women's participation at the highest decision-making level has fallen over the last decade. This development was in marked contrast with increased female representation in the country's representative bodies.

In this context, it is important to briefly reflect on the role of the armed forces in Cuban society. Of the twenty-four Politburo members, seven (25 percent) are high-ranking army officers. They include Fidel Castro, the commander-in-chief; his brother Raúl, the minister of defense; four generals; and one major. Similarly, on the party's Central Committee, active and retired military officers hold more than a quarter of the seats.[48] These figures demonstrate that the armed forces are well represented in the inner sanctum of power. Cuba has only one woman who serves as a general. Women are disadvantaged in their career advancement because they were not assigned to such overseas combat missions as Angola.[49] It is easy to see that exclusion from top military careers is one of the structural impediments to women's advancement in the party ranks.

Concepción Campa, one of the two exceptional women who did make it into the top party hierarchy, conveyed a sense of surprise at being permitted into the inner sanctum of power:

I must confess to you that, to my surprise, I was elected a member of the Politburo of the Central Committee at the [1991] party congress. I had been part of the organizing committee of this party congress, together with other scientists and specialists. For me it was a surprise, a real surprise that resulted in a host of sentiments. The first feeling that I experienced was that I was not deserving of this election; I felt that I was not worthy of this distinction. The other feeling was that I had a great responsibility in assuming this appointment. [It was] a very, very great responsibility, which led to another sentiment; the feeling that life suddenly forced me to grow in a very abrupt way. If you know a little about the personality of someone dedicated to the sciences, this is not exactly equivalent to a person dedicated to communication, to social work, [or] to political work. These are not things that coincide in general with the life and work of a scientist. Instead, one remains isolated, absorbed in thought, one's nose to the grindstone, as [José] Martí said. But this is it. It is not one's strength to speak in public, to transmit ideas, except in some congress or some scientific event where we scientists talk of our topics. Social and public communication is not the strength of scientists. Thus, I felt that, apart from not deserving it and in addition to it being a great responsibility, I had to grow, grow in a world that not only was not my strength but that I never could have dreamt of being in.

Then came the Fifth Party Congress, at which I was reelected to the Politburo. . . . I sensed a responsibility because I felt and continue to feel that I hold a position not based on my merits but [that I am] representing a whole sector. I feel I am representing two things that are sacred for me. I feel that I am representing the sciences and the work of many Cuban scientists who work day and night. But I also feel that I am representing my gender as a woman. This is also for me something very sacred. To represent my gender as a woman is for me as sacred as representing my profession.[50]

Campa projected a sense of honor in serving on the Politburo and the challenge of living up to the importance of such a position. She also expressed a clear gender consciousness. Interestingly, Campa did not feel the need to defend women's rights on the Politburo: "It seems to me that in Cuba this role [of taking up women's rights issues] is played well by the Federation of Cuban Women. The support one could give individually pales in comparison to the support that the Federation of Cuban Women can give in this regard. I belong to the FMC's national committee, and I believe this is where this is taken care of. . . . In the Politburo it is not necessary to play this role, because a situation in which one would need to defend one thing or another from a gender perspective does not arise."[51] Campa's position absolves the party from its responsibility to address gender inequalities and locates the duty for defending women's rights in the FMC.

Cuban feminists with whom I spoke tended to be critical of the party's efforts to change the gender composition of its leadership. Many gave pessimistic assessments for the possibility of strengthened gender equality in the party ranks. As one source emphasized, "I don't think that the membership or the party leadership has a gender consciousness nor do the female party members, which is most disturbing."[52] The source refers here to substantive gender equality, which requires a change in consciousness, acknowledging that relations between women and men need to be reconstituted, as opposed to the affirmative-action measures party and state officials favor to strengthen women's formal participation in decision-making.

Additional factors at play explain why few women hold leadership positions in the party and the mass organizations. Mavis Álvarez, a member of the Small Farmers' Association's directorate, offered this perspective:

> As the leadership levels rise, the responsibilities for these officials are greater. I tell you this as a woman who has spent thirty years in the national directorate of my organization [ANAP]. The responsibilities are tremendous, quite large. Thus, in general, a woman has a certain prejudice against holding positions of great responsibility that take her away from giving attention to the family and complicate her life extraordinarily. Also, you must take into account the conditions in Cuba. In the Cuban economy it is the woman who suffers most from the burden of the scarcity of food products and of household appliances that would make her domestic work and caring for the family easier. . . . So when you pick a peasant woman and you tell her to take a position in the farmer's movement in her community, this complicates her life. But when you tell her to move to a municipal leadership position, you complicate her life even more, and when you promote a woman to the provincial leadership—because here enters the housing problem, which is another very difficult problem in Cuba—and this woman has her house in the cooperative with her family, with her children, it is very difficult to break with this reality. Because we don't have the conditions in the country to say, "Look, we'll give you a house here in the province so that you and your family can live here and you can dedicate yourself to this." She can't move. If you put her at the national level. . . . We have *compañeras* here who are national-level officials that have been living in a hostel for four, five years.[53]

Considering this reality, it is easy to understand why many women are averse to accepting the responsibilities that come with a leadership position. Also, as Concepción Campa argued "women need to lose the fear of working and participating in politics." In her view, it is "maybe more difficult for a

Table 4.10. Women's Participation in the Leadership Structures of the Communist Youth Movement (UJC), 1996–1999

| | Percentage of Women | |
Structure and Membership	1996	1999
Politburo	19.2	27.8
National Committee	n/a	30.8
Leadership of Provincial Committees	10.7	13.3
Leadership of Municipal Committees	n/a	32.2
1st Secretaries	19.1	19.5
Membership	44.9	47.1

Source: UJC–Departamento de Organización

woman to get up and to talk than for a man. It is less traditional for women to do this."[54] In addition, for positions at the highest level, the requirements are so demanding that few women have the qualifications to compete effectively. Female leaders frequently pointed out that the situation is not different in Europe or the United States, where, with the exception of the Scandinavian countries, few women consistently occupy top leadership positions.

The argument concerning the lack of qualified female leaders appears weak if we examine the gender composition of the communist youth organization (UJC), which represented a main source for the recruitment of party leaders. Otto Rivero, the head of the UJC, maintained that "more than half of the people joining the party come from the Youth Movement."[55] Within the UJC, women constitute close to half of the membership. Significantly, the two highest-ranking bodies of the party youth organization, the Politburo and the National Committee, have a membership of about one-third women.

Rivero maintained that women were sought-after members. "We hold the view that women fulfill our tasks better than men. They are more serious, more competent, more responsible, and they also achieve a greater level of influence in their work with young people."[56] About half of all university students are affiliated with the movement. According to Rivero, "Of every two university students in the country, one is a militant in the Youth Movement."[57] Thus, the educational elite is represented in the party's youth organization.

The number of female leaders in the UJC's national bodies is noticeable when compared to the gender composition of the party's leadership. The data indicate that women in the party hierarchy reach a glass ceiling as they rise through the ranks. Although they hold leadership positions in the UJC, they are not as readily accepted into high party positions as their male counterparts.

Conclusion

Female legislators in Cuba do not get together as a group to discuss common issues confronting them or to design strategies on how to advance gender equality. "Women get together in the federation or in other environments, but in the assembly we have never gotten together."[58] This contrasts with the experience of female deputies in many Latin American parliaments, who are generally organized as a group within their political parties. In addition, women in a number of countries (e.g., El Salvador, Panama, and Uruguay) have formed alliances across ideological boundaries in an effort to change dominant gender relations. Cuban legislators leave this mission to party officials and the Women's Federation but do not consider it a priority task for themselves.[59]

The evidence presented in this chapter supports the view that Cuba has not made as much progress in achieving gender equality in political decision-making as some of the official data would point to and that women continue to be largely excluded from the most important decision-making bodies. The Cuban experience indicates that female participation in a party of the revolutionary left does not necessarily translate into strong representation in the most important decision-making structures.

In the Cuban system, power is located in the Communist party. Few women are to be found in the Politburo and the Central Committee, with women's representation declining in the past few years. This confirms that Cuban women hold little decision-making power. The failure of the Cuban Communist party to incorporate more women into its leadership is evidence that the revolutionary authorities' commitment to gender equality is limited. Interestingly, as the number of female party members increases, their numbers in key leadership structures decline. Further, we find important differences between state and party structures. In Cuba's Poder Popular, women's participation increases from the municipal assemblies to the National Assembly, while this relationship is reversed in the case of the party structures. The excellent gender balance of the National Assembly demonstrates that authorities could successfully increase female representation levels if they were inclined to do so.

At the governmental level, there is recognition that gender equality needs to be strengthened, and important initiatives have been undertaken to do so. Recent gender initiatives included the Council of State's evaluation of the status of formal gender equity in Cuba's ministries. As a result of the evaluation, the council issued a directive to the heads of all administrative state structures, which stated that any forthcoming proposals for high-level administrative positions have to be balanced in terms of gender. Thus, for every position, one of two candidates has to be a woman.[60] Further, Cuba's 2002 Plan of Action, designed as a follow-up to the Beijing conference, emphasized that several ministries and organizations should include gender in their training programs.[61] Among them were the Ministries of Sugar, Education, and Tourism as well as Cuban Radio and two mass organizations, the CTC and ANAP.

In general, Cuban officials are reluctant to acknowledge the need for corrective measures in order to advance women in politics, while making obvious behind-the-scene adjustments to ensure a favorable gender composition in selected decision-making bodies. This deprives societal forces favoring gender equality of the mobilizing power of public discussion. It preempts coalition-building, which could bring pressure to bear on the party to make its decision-making bodies more representative or to have a public discussion on the differences in the gender composition of local versus national government structures. Without a public dialogue, prevailing *machista* attitudes, which impede women's advancement, will not be challenged. The fact that Cuban women hold little political power needs to be openly addressed for societal consciousness to change, a necessary condition for substantive gender equality to emerge. Ironically, the Cuban leadership, which professes support for gender equality, undermines its own goal of transforming society. Whereas the leadership has the power to institute measures that strengthen formal equality, any substantive change requires that the common Cuban citizen be in support of gender equality, something that requires consciousness raising.

Gender Equality and Electoral Politics

The 2002–2003 National Elections

It is our responsibility to organize this [expression of the] people's will, search for a composition, [and] search for representativeness. And these are the candidacies. We neither invent names, nor do we bring out a name that occurred to us and get together in a closed office and say: "Well, let's include Aidita, let's include Alfredo, or let's include this one." Instead, starting with these long lists, we begin to form the candidate projects in a process of successive approximations.

Eduardo Freire

Eduardo Freire, president of the National Candidate Commission, provides in the statement above a snapshot of the complex process the commission went through in order to arrive at the final candidate lists for the 2002–2003 national elections.[1] This selection process is part of Cuban electoral dynamics, which are the topic of this chapter. The Cuban Communist party plays a decisive role in the election process. Cuban officials recognize the problematic of one party controlling the electoral process and insist that the party does not formally participate in the election process. Roberto Díaz, minister of justice and head of the National Election Commission, presented the official position: "For an electoral process in a one-party system to be truly democratic, well, simply put, from its origins it was conceived that the party should not have any institutional participation in the elections. This does not mean that the party militants cannot, like any other citizen, participate under equal conditions. . . . [However] the fact of being a party militant does not give him any prerogative."[2] These assurances notwithstanding, Cuban practice shows extensive party involvement.

The 2002–2003 elections constituted an important opportunity to provide a window into the Cuban election process. This chapter complements the previous analysis by giving a detailed account of a specific election. Whereas comprehensive studies have been published that examine the Cuban elections, these studies lack a gender perspective.[3] I begin with a look at the candidate nomination process and then present detailed election results for the municipal and national level. The focus of this chapter will be on examining the gender composition of the various assemblies.

The Nomination Process for People's Power Candidates

The National Candidate Commission (Comisión Nacional de Candidaturas, or CNC) oversees the process of selecting the candidates at the national level. The commission consists of representatives of the Cuban mass organizations, with the Cuban Confederation of Workers (Central de Trabajadores de Cuba, or CTC) playing the leading role. Eduardo Freire emphasized that the CTC is given the leading role because "the strength of the revolution and the strength of any country are its workers, who create the resources, the goods, the services of a country. Without workers, there would be no country. Thus, this is the leading force of a society, as much in capitalism as in socialism."[4]

By law, each mass organization has the right to nominate representatives to the commission. In 2002–2003 Ernesto Freire, the CTC's secretary general, headed the commission, a role he had also played in the previous election. The other eleven members consisted of two representatives each from the Cuban Women's Federation (FMC), the Small Farmers' Association (ANAP), the Neighborhood Committees (CDRs), the Federation of University Students (FEU), and the Federation of High-School Students (FEEM). Completing the commission's makeup was a second CTC representative. The representatives on the commission were "of course from the national leadership of the [respective] organizations."[5]

According to Freire, half of the commission's membership consisted of women. The representatives of the FEU and the FEEM were to ensure that the youth perspective received appropriate attention. It is interesting that the Federation of High School Students had membership status, considering that most of the FEEM membership is not of voting age. The FEEM representatives recognized that this fact limited the organization's role to some degree. Ana Margarita Morejón, the FEEM representative on the commission, affirmed that "the case of the FEEM is somewhat particular, because in the instance of the National Assembly, the Cuban Parliament, [a candidate] needs to be eighteen years old. Since the majority of the FEEM students leave the organization before they complete the age of eighteen," the FEEM representatives cannot advance candidates from their own organization for national office.[6]

The candidate commissions exist at the national, provincial, and municipal levels. Their main task is to draw up candidate lists for the representative structures at the regional and national level, thus fulfilling the task the voters play at the local level. As discussed, candidates to the municipal assemblies are selected by voters in electoral districts divided into smaller nomination areas. In determining the provincial and national lists, the commissions "work hand in hand with the plenums of the mass organizations at all three levels. . . . The work of the plenums is combined with massive consultations at the place of work and in the neighborhood, culminating in the final decision by the municipal delegates as to who should be candidates" at the provincial and national level.[7]

The mass organizations hold plenary sessions to select pre-candidates, normally nominating their own officials and members. At times, candidates are selected who are not members but are considered advocates for the organization's interests. For example, Leonardo Martínez, the president of one of the National Assembly's key bodies, the Commission on Productive Activities, was originally elected to Parliament as a candidate nominated by the CTC. Martínez's commission decided issues of great relevance to the farming community, however. In light of this, both the union and the small farmers decided to nominate him for the 1997–98 election cycle. Martínez affirmed: "ANAP nominated me apart from the union that kept me in its proposal. . . . We have developed many important topics in the commission, which I preside over, that have an enormous impact on the peasantry."[8]

The task of selecting the final candidate lists for the national and provincial assemblies is enormous. In the 2002–2003 elections 57,340 candidates were proposed in 860 meetings sponsored by Cuba's social movements.[9] The lists generated by the mass organizations were pared down by the Candidate Commissions, which sought to ensure that the final list of candidates was representative in terms of gender, professional background, and other characteristics. Among the many people who were nominated, there were about 2,000 candidates for the National Assembly who were of "national interest." Out of those, about 140 were selected. A similar number were to represent "provincial interests," with up to 50 percent of the remaining positions being filled by candidates coming from the municipal assemblies.[10] Whereas the provincial candidate commissions nominated candidates for both the regional and national levels, the National Commission nominated pre-candidates only for the National Assembly.

Once the final lists of the pre-candidates, with input from the mass organizations and the Candidate Commissions, had been constituted, they were presented to the respective municipal assemblies. The municipal assemblies then voted either to approve the list or to reject it partially or completely. Although the lists were generally approved, the local elected representatives held ultimate authority in determining the candidates. Eduardo Lara, who served as an advisor on constitutional matters to the National Assembly, emphasized that it is "the municipal assembly which plays the role in our country that political parties play in other countries. Since we don't have electoral parties, the representatives of the people, those elected to the municipal assemblies, [officially] nominate the candidate proposed by the Candidate Commission."[11]

Up to 50 percent of the provincial and national delegates who were included in the final lists came by law from the pool of the previously elected municipal delegates. The idea behind this was to ensure that local problems and perspectives were well understood at the national level. National Assembly member María Josefa Ruíz advanced this view: "Someone who is in the municipal assembly shares life with those who elected him, with the voters of the district. He lives with them and knows in a direct way the problems that exist in this little part."[12] This feature of the Cuban electoral system elevates the importance of local elections. Lara pointed out that "when someone is nominated [to the municipal assembly], the people already are aware that he has the credentials to serve as a municipal delegate, a provincial delegate, or a national delegate."[13]

Although the National Assembly meets only twice a year for a few days, those delegates who serve simultaneously in a municipal assembly and the Parliament have a considerable workload. As discussed, the Parliament's work takes place mostly in the ten permanent commissions. About half of the assembly members serve on one of the commissions. In his rich, detailed study of People's Power, Peter Roman has emphasized that many prominent Parliament members "who have high government positions or other prominent careers have little time to participate in the commissions, unless they serve as commission officers, a circumstance that points to the relative importance of the less prominent deputies, especially the *de base* deputies (those who are also municipal delegates), in carrying out the functions of the National Assembly."[14] Compared to other parliaments throughout the world, the Cuban National Assembly has limited importance in the country's decision-making process. Roman has pointed out that the Cuban Parliament does not determine long-term policy since this is the prerogative of the party. Furthermore, whereas "individual deputies may propose laws, legislative initiatives have not come from deputies. They have neither the time (since most are not professional politicians, they continue working at their regular jobs) nor the staff nor the necessary support to give them sufficient independence. Thus, the National Assembly serves more as a consultative than an initiating body, where proposed legislation is submitted for review, modification, and approval."[15] Cubans do not attribute to their Parliament the significance usually accorded to a national legislature. María Josefa Ruíz's statement confirms this: "[We have] an assembly where one can discuss, debate everything and make a proposal to solve a problem. . . . [However], it is not the assembly that directly resolves the problem. But it has its weight."[16]

At the local level, depending on the neighborhood's size, a minimum of two and a maximum of eight candidates are nominated for each municipal council seat. In the first round of the October 19, 2002 elections to the municipal assemblies, 32,585 candidates were nominated. Of those, 8,144 (25 percent) were women and 24,432 (75 percent) were men. Representing Cuba's youth sector, 3,223 candidates were younger than thirty years old.[17] Thus, there were on average three candidates for every one of the 14,946 delegate seats to be determined. Following the municipal elections, the candidate commissions consulted with the members of a particular town council in order to propose a president and a vice president to chair the council.[18] The local candidate commission chaired this event and formally handed over power to the elected president. This was the last stage in the work of the candidate commission at the local level.

As discussed in chapter 4, considerably fewer women tend to be nominated at the local level compared with the provincial/national level. This was also the case in the 2002–2003 elections. Ana María Moreno, a member of the municipal council of Arroyo Naranjo who also served on the Health, Sports, and Environment Commission of the National Assembly, noted that women were passed over even though they demonstrated their problem-solving and leadership capabilities on a daily basis:

At the local level, people think at times that women will not fix the problems. Certainly, the woman continues to be the one who has the most weight in the household. Sometimes a person says, "She can't do it because she is a woman. She must take care of the house and her husband." Well, practice has demonstrated the opposite. The woman continues to be the boss in the household, as we say. And she is very responsible in taking care of the work [of the town council]. Very few women start in these positions and don't finish their term. At times, more men resign than women. Socially, women have gained due to this [commitment].[19]

Moreno recognized the gender bias prevailing at the local level, while insisting that things were changing. However, it is evident that societal change needs to be helped along, in the form of concrete measures favoring women, in order for female candidates to have a better chance at success. As discussed, it is due to measures of positive discrimination that the selection process for the provincial and national levels produce a more balanced gender composition. The difference in female representation across the three levels of government indicate that there is a considerable gap in how the average voter values the normative goal of achieving gender equality in decision-making, compared to the members of the candidate commissions or the leadership of the mass organizations and the Communist party.

The Local and National Elections

Cuban elections are greatly decentralized to facilitate high turnout. Citizen involvement in the election process itself is extensive. In 2002–2003 about 184,000 citizens formed part of the election commissions of the 36,927 poll places. This way an electorate of 8.3 million could be easily accommodated. On October 20, 2002, almost 8 million voters, close to 96 percent of the electorate, went to the polls. In the first round of the elections, 13,563 delegates were elected. Of those, 6,079 (22.7 percent) were women, and about half of the new deputies (6,493) had served in municipal governments in the preceding term. A considerable number of the newly elected representatives (920 or 6.76 percent) were less than thirty years old.[20]

In order to be elected in the first round, a candidate needed more than 50 percent of the valid votes. In those localities where none of the candidates obtained an absolute majority, a runoff election was held on October 27. In this second round, 1,232,690 people, representing 91.5 percent of the eligible voters, chose candidates in 1,370 electoral precincts that were located in 124 municipalities. Since candidates in three precincts received the same number of votes, only 1,367 delegates were elected. In the remaining three precincts, a third round of elections had to be conducted on October 30 to determine the winners.[21]

Table 5.1. Election Results to the Municipal Assemblies, 2002

Provinces	Registered Voters	Votes Deposited	%	Blank Ballots	%	Spoiled Ballots	%
Pinar del Río	543,106	527,031	97.04	20,861	3.96	10,900	2.07
La Habana	540,664	532,710	98.53	17,634	3.31	23,799	4.47
Ciudad de la Habana	1,696,118	1,578,468	93.06	41,898	2.65	60,916	3.86
Matanzas	514,655	495,811	96.34	14,430	2.91	18,013	3.63
Villa Clara	623,056	601,835	96.59	20,743	3.45	17,865	2.97
Cienfuegos	298,800	290,079	97.08	9,728	3.35	8,871	3.06
Sancti Spíritus	357,894	344,688	96.31	7,970	2.31	7,170	2.08
Ciego de Ávila	303,496	291,766	96.14	6,467	2.22	5,246	1.80
Camagüey	577,587	550,931	95.38	14,628	2.66	13,478	2.45
Las Tunas	382,025	373,098	97.66	8,509	2.28	5,187	1.39
Holguín	762,301	730,099	95.78	25,105	3.44	12,036	1.65
Granma	587,630	570,729	97.12	13,038	2.28	6,355	1.11
Santiago de Cuba	751,197	714,701	95.14	13,396	1.87	8,070	1.13
Guantánamo	352,245	336,753	95.60	6,328	1.88	3,716	1.10
Isla de la Juventud	62,174	59,362	95.48	1,841	3.10	1,248	2.10
Total	8,352,948	7,998,061	95.75	222,576	2.78	202,870	2.54

Source: National Election Commission

As in most previous municipal elections, the city of Havana and Havana Province had the highest incidence of blank and spoiled ballots, with 7.8 percent and 6.5 percent, respectively. This rate compared to a national average of 5.3 percent. Even if we assume that most of these ballots were left blank or were spoiled as a sign of protest, the total number of invalid votes was relatively insignificant. Furthermore, at least some voters spoiled their ballots by accident, as happens in elections across the world.

In the January 19, 2003, elections to the National Assembly, all 609 candidates were elected. As we know, under the Cuban system there was only one candidate per seat at the national level. Thus, the only way for a voter to express dissatisfaction was to abstain from endorsing a specific candidate. A rejection of the government in general could only be manifested by leaving the ballot blank or by spoiling it.

According to official data, Fidel Castro was reelected with 99 percent of the votes cast in Santiago de Cuba, where he headed the list of candidates representing "national interests." His brother, Raúl, did even better, receiving 99.75 percent in the same electoral district. Throughout the country, only 24 candidates got less than 90 percent of the vote. A female candidate in old town Havana obtained the lowest approval with 85.15 percent. As noted, among the new members of Parliament was Juan Miguel González, Elián's father, who had been elected in his home town of Cárdenas.[22] Such vote totals raise immediate suspicion in the eyes of a Western observer. Yet there is no reason to believe that the vote is manipulated in any way. In particular, the secrecy of the vote is strictly observed.

As table 5.2 shows, participation rates in Cuba tend to be very high, consistently above 90 percent. As noted, the Cuban system encourages high turnout. For example, Cuba has an automatic voting registration system. The high voter participation is particularly noticeable if one takes into account that voting in Cuba is not obligatory. Roberto Díaz emphasized that for voters who choose to abstain, "there are no consequences from a penal point of view, or in terms of their work. From a political point of view there are also no consequences for someone who doesn't vote, because this is not registered anywhere."[23] In reality, however, there was considerable social pressure for people to vote. Voting is considered a patriotic duty. Neighbors notice who stays at home on election day, and election workers go from house to house to encourage those who have not yet voted to do so.

While social pressure is a factor in the high turnout, it does not explain the astonishingly high degree of voter approval all candidates receive. The fact that even some relatively unknown candidates obtain such a high vote total can be attributed to one of the idiosyncrasies of the Cuban system—the "unity vote."

Table 5.2. Election Results to the National Assembly, 2003

Provinces	Votes Deposited	Valid Votes	%	Unified Vote	%	Selective Vote	%	Blank Ballots	%	Spoiled Ballots	%
Pinar del Río	530,684	507,361	95.61	473,085	93.24	34,276	6.76	20,644	3.89	2,679	0.50
La Habana	540,541	513,581	95.01	473,209	92.14	40,372	7.86	19,840	3.67	7,120	1.32
Ciudad de la Habana	1,620,554	1,536,105	94.79	1,352,919	88.07	183,186	11.93	55,234	3.41	29,215	1.80
Matanzas	499,146	480,405	96.25	429,691	89.44	50,714	10.56	13,749	2.75	4,992	1.00
Villa Clara	608,418	580,694	95.44	532,125	91.64	48,569	8.36	22,005	3.62	5,719	0.94
Cienfuegos	292,054	279,277	95.63	254,476	91.12	24,801	8.88	10,143	3.47	2,634	0.90
Sancti Spíritus	346,352	334,524	96.58	308,325	92.17	26,199	7.83	9,443	2.73	2,385	0.69
Ciego de Ávila	297,601	289,359	97.23	265,384	91.71	23,975	8.29	6,936	2.33	1,306	0.44
Camagüey	565,072	546,260	96.67	498,698	91.29	47,562	8.71	14,842	2.63	3,970	0.70
Las Tunas	373,702	363,540	97.28	339,987	93.52	23,553	6.48	9,023	2.41	1,139	0.30
Holguín	739,231	708,344	95.82	654,945	92.46	53,399	7.54	27,233	3.68	3,654	0.49
Granma	577,077	563,932	97.72	527,786	93.59	36,146	6.41	11,760	2.04	1,385	0.24
Santiago de Cuba	727,679	710,687	97.66	662,929	93.28	47,758	6.72	14,528	2.00	2,464	0.34
Guantánamo	338,505	331,446	97.91	305,531	92.18	25,915	7.82	6,320	1.87	739	0.22
Isla de la Juventud	60,535	58,383	96.45	49,770	85.25	8,613	14.75	1,690	2.79	462	0.76
Total	8,117,151	7,803,898	96.14	7,128,860	91.35	675,038	8.65	243,390	3.00	69,863	0.86

Source: National Election Commission

As discussed, Cubans tend to heed the call of the leadership, in particular that of Fidel Castro, to cast a "unified" as opposed to a "selective" vote.[24] In 2003 more than 90 percent of the voters exercised the unity vote option, with the city of Havana experiencing the most significant incidence of selective voting with 12 percent. Thus, the voters in the capital were less likely to follow the advice of the leadership than the electorate in the rest of the country. Combined with the higher incidence of invalid ballots, one can draw the conclusion that *habaneros* were somewhat more dissatisfied with their government or at least more likely to express it.

The Gender Composition of Cuba's Poder Popular

The 2002–2003 elections confirmed the arguments presented earlier concerning women's participation in Cuba's decision-making structures. Although women made progress overall, the already existing differences in the gender composition of the local versus national legislative bodies continued to grow.

At the municipal level, female participation increased somewhat from 21 to over 23 percent. However, the data presented in table 5.3 demonstrate that there were significant differences among the country's provinces. Pinar del Río's municipal assemblies averaged only 17 percent female participation, whereas the city of Havana had close to 35 percent.

Table 5.3. Gender Composition of the Municipal Assemblies by Province, 2002

Provinces	Women	%	Men	%	Total
Pinar del Río	218	16.96	1,067	83.04	1,285
La Habana	284	26.03	807	73.97	1,091
Ciudad de la Habana	546	34.84	1,021	65.16	1,567
Matanzas	256	27.68	669	72.32	925
Villa Clara	280	21.29	1,035	78.71	1,315
Cienfuegos	186	30.15	431	69.85	617
Sancti Spíritus	164	22.94	551	77.06	715
Ciego de Ávila	146	21.79	524	78.21	670
Camagüey	224	22.56	769	77.44	993
Las Tunas	181	22.63	619	77.37	800
Holguín	252	17.12	1,220	82.88	1,472
Granma	236	18.66	1,029	81.34	1,265
Santiago de Cuba	320	24.22	1,001	75.78	1,321
Guantánamo	174	21.14	649	78.86	823
Isla de la Juventud	26	29.89	61	70.11	87
Total	3,493	23.37	11,453	76.63	14,946

Source: Calculated based on data in *Granma*, Nov. 4, 2002, 3

Table 5.4. Gender Composition of the Provincial Assembly of Havana City, 2003

Municipality	Women	Men	% of Female Candidates
Playa	4	8	33.33
Plaza	2	9	18.18
Centro Habana	2	9	18.18
La Habana Vieja	2	4	33.33
Regla	0	3	00.00
La Habana del Este	4	8	33.33
Guanabacoa	1	6	14.28
San Miguel del Padrón	4	7	36.36
Diez de Octubre	6	9	40.00
Cerro	3	6	33.33
Marianao	4	5	44.44
La Lisa	5	4	55.55
Boyeros	5	7	41.60
Arroyo Naranjo	6	8	42.85
Cotorro	1	4	20.00
Total	49	97	33.56

Source: Calculated based on data in *Tribuna de la Habana*, Dec. 8, 2002, p. 4

The results for Pinar del Río were particularly interesting, considering that until 2003 the province could boast that its Communist party apparatus was headed by a woman, the only female first secretary in the country.[25] There was no discernible pattern in how the voters of a specific province allocated their support for female candidates at the local as opposed to the regional or national level. Whereas Pinar del Río had the lowest level of support for women at the municipal level, it had the third highest at the national level.[26] Similarly, the town councils in Holguín Province had a gender composition that was barely better than those in Pinar del Río (17 percent), yet at the national level it reached close to 40 percent.

As in the past, female participation rates at the provincial level were significantly higher than those in the municipalities. Havana City was the exception. It was above the national average, with 35 percent female representation in the capital's town councils but achieved less than 34 percent at the provincial level. Across municipalities that formed the provincial assembly of Havana City, there was considerable variance. For example, Regla did not have a single female delegate, while a majority of the delegates in La Lisa were female.

Table 5.5 shows the contribution the various provinces made to the Parliament's gender composition. The province of Ciego de Ávila sent an equal number of women and men to Parliament, whereas Granma remained far below the national average with barely 20 percent female representation. San-

Table 5.5. Gender Composition of the National Assembly by Province, 2003

Provinces	Women	%	Men	%	Total
Pinar del Río	16	41.03	23	58.97	39
La Habana	16	38.10	26	61.90	42
Ciudad de la Habana	41	36.60	71	63.40	112
Matanzas	14	35.00	26	65.00	40
Villa Clara	16	36.36	28	63.64	44
Cienfuegos	7	30.43	16	69.57	23
Sancti Spíritus	9	36.00	16	64.00	25
Ciego de Ávila	13	50.00	13	50.00	26
Camagüey	21	46.67	24	53.33	45
Las Tunas	8	29.63	19	70.37	27
Holguín	21	38.89	33	61.11	54
Granma	9	20.45	35	79.55	44
Santiago de Cuba	15	28.85	37	71.15	52
Guantánamo	12	37.50	20	62.50	32
Isla de la Juventud	1	35.00	3	75.00	4
Total	219	35.96	390	64.04	609

Source: Calculated based on data in *Granma*, Dec. 2, 2002, pp. 5–7

tiago de Cuba also stayed considerably below the national average. The Candidate Commission assigned a number of famous male politicians, including the Castro brothers, as candidates of "national interest" to Santiago. This might explain why the gender composition there was not more equal.[27]

The gender composition of Cuba's Poder Popular improved substantially in the 2002–2003 elections. The increase was smallest at the municipal level, where female participation increased from 21 to over 23 percent. At the provincial level, on the other hand, women achieved a historic high with almost 38 percent, increasing their participation by almost 9 percent. The results were equally impressive at the national level. The new Parliament was composed of 219 female deputies (36 percent) out of a total of 609 members, a jump of over 8 percent.

Conclusion

In the wake of the 2002–2003 elections, the continued difference in the level of female representation between the local versus the regional and national level was further evidence for a key argument presented in this study; namely, that the high female participation rates in the regional and national legislatures were the result of the effective implementation of measures of positive discrimination. Without the social engineering of the candidate commissions, women would have made little progress in increasing their presence in Cuba's

Table 5.6. Gender Composition of Cuba's Poder Popular, 2003

Level	Women	%	Men	%	Total
Municipal Assemblies	3,493	23.4	11,453	76.6	14,946
Provincial Assemblies	451	37.6	748	62.4	1,199
National Assembly	219	35.9	390	64.1	609

Source: National Election Commission

decision-making bodies. Interestingly, this meant that the body chosen in the least democratic manner had the highest percentage of women.[28]

The 2002–2003 election process provided evidence that much remained to be done in Cuba to change prevailing gender relations and supported the argument concerning the unintended consequences of Cuban government policies. The official emphasis on the favorable gender balance of the National Assembly and the rejection of quotas was counterproductive. It permitted officials to "correct" the results of grassroots democracy through the input of the candidate commissions without having to acknowledge that the gender consciousness of the Cuban voter was not particularly well developed. Thus, instead of an open national campaign addressing these issues, discussion was restricted to "elite" circles. The Cuban government could claim exceptional success in the international arena by pointing to the gender balance it had achieved at the national level while papering over problems at the local level. Furthermore, and most significantly, the high levels of female participation in the National Assembly raises the question why the party leadership has done so little to improve the unequal gender composition of the Politburo and the Central Committee.

Conclusion

Gender Equality and Democratization

Few illusions are held about a switch to Western-style market democracy or Eastern-style
perestroika-glasnost, each being seen as a potential threat to women's gains. No oppositional
groupings of import have emerged within the broader political structure, either to the party
or to the mass organizations; there is no rival to the FMC, feminist or otherwise.

Jean Stubbs, "Revolutionizing Women, Family, and Power"

A decade after knowledgeable observers predicted that the Cuban system of government would emerge essentially unchanged from the crisis of the early 1990s, we know that they have been proven right by history. The Cuban Women's Federation as well as the Communist party remained basically unchallenged, hegemonic forces.[1] The continued legitimacy of the regime was rooted in the revolution's record. The significant post-1959 accomplishments continued to have more weight in the eyes of the citizens than the obvious hardship people endured. The revolution was frayed on more than the edges, but no credible alternatives were in sight. Change was most likely to come from within.

The Cuban government was rightfully proud of the country's record in guaranteeing basic economic and social rights for all citizens. Its policies had been particularly successful in extending these rights to women. Few countries in the world could point to a better long-term record in providing access to health care and education for their female population, even though the system has been under serious strain since the early 1990s.

Women's political participation was also respectable. Women did actively participate in the political process as voters, candidates, and officeholders. In some instances, particularly in the case of women's representation in the National Assembly, women did exceedingly well. However, the high level of formal political participation could not hide the fact that women held limited decision-making power.

In order to assess the Cuban record objectively, we need to put it in a regional and international context. Over the last decade an international consensus has emerged around the call for equal participation of women and men

Table 6.1. Gender Composition of the World's Parliaments, 2006 (Single or Lower House)

Region	Percentage of Female MPs	Percentage of Male MPs
Nordic Countries	40.0	60.0
Americas	19.6	80.4
Europe OSCE (Nordic countries included)	19.0	81.0
Europe OSCE (Nordic countries not included)	16.9	83.1
Sub-Saharan Africa	16.4	83.6
Asia	16.3	83.7
Pacific	12.0	88.0
Arab States	8.3	91.7
World Average	16.6	83.4

Source: Inter-Parliamentary Union (February 2006)

in parliamentary decision-making. The Platform of Action, a main document that focused on issues of gender and women's rights as key objectives to be pursued by national and international actors, resulted from the 1995 Fourth World Conference on Women held in Beijing. The Beijing Platform exhorted governments to ensure a minimum level of representation for women, referred to as a "critical mass"—generally considered to be 30 percent. More recent initiatives have formed around 50-50 campaigns, advocating a fully gender-balanced parliament.[2] Yet formal gender parity in political decision-making is still in the distant future.

At the beginning of 2006, less than 17 percent of the world's parliamentarians were women. The Nordic countries stood out with more than twice the world average. Across the world there were considerable regional variations, with the Arab countries reporting about 8 percent and the Americas reaching close to 20 percent, yet very few countries come close to approaching gender parity in the composition of their parliaments. Significantly, the percentage of parliaments with less than 10 percent female representation had dropped from 63 percent in 1995 to 37 percent in 2005.[3] There were still eight nations that had no female representation in their parliaments whatsoever.

In terms of national records, only Rwanda, the Scandinavian countries, and Holland had a similar or better parliamentary gender balance than Cuba. In 2005 Rwanda had almost achieved gender parity with 48.8 percent women. It was followed by Sweden (45.3 percent), Norway (37.9 percent), and Finland (37.5 percent), countries where women parliamentarians were close to being on equal footing with men. These leaders in women's formal political participation were followed by Denmark and the Netherlands, which approached

Table 6.2. Gender Composition of the Revolutionary Left's Leadership Structures, 2001

	Women	%	Men	%
Cuba–PCC	2	8.3	22	91.7
Nicaragua–FSLN	6	40.0	9	60.0
El Salvador–FMLN	6	40.0	9	60.0

Source: Partido Comunista de Cuba; Frente Sandinista de Liberación Nacional; Frente Far-abundo Martí para la Liberación Nacional

37 percent. Spain (36 percent) and Germany (with close to 33 percent) also had favorable gender balances in their parliaments. The United States (14.9 percent) and most European Union countries, on the other hand, including France (12.2 percent), Italy (11.5 percent), and the United Kingdom (18.1 percent), had considerably fewer women holding seats in parliament.

Regionally, only Costa Rica (35.1 percent) and Argentina (33.7 percent) had a level of female representation similar to the one in Cuba. Mexico (22.6 percent), Chile (12.5 percent), and Brazil (8.6 percent) were much more representative of Latin America's parliamentary gender composition.[4] As noted, however, the limited decision-making power of Cuba's National Assembly makes the Cuban record less remarkable.

Whereas Cuba had a high level of female representation in its National Assembly, this was not the case for the national leadership structures of the Communist party, in which power was located. The gender composition of the PCC's leadership is best compared with those of other revolutionary movements in the region that have evolved into political parties.

Examining the case of Central America, we find that the PCC did not compare well with its sister parties. For example, in 2001 both the National Directorate of the Sandinista party in Nicaragua and the Political Commission of the Farabundo Martí National Liberation Front in El Salvador had almost five times the percentage of women in their highest national decision-making body. In both cases, the parties had established quotas to ensure adequate levels of women's participation. Thus, the failure of the Cuban Communist party to incorporate more women into its leadership was evidence that the government's commitment to gender equality was limited. In the final analysis, it was the lack of support from the party leadership that kept women out of the top decision-making positions. The excellent gender composition of the National Assembly was evidence that the authorities could successfully increase female representation levels if they were inclined to do so.

The leadership's position, in turn, reflected a societal consciousness that had yet to fully embrace substantive gender equality. What Cuba needed was an open discussion concerning gender equality in political decision-making.

The policy of correcting gender imbalances behind the scenes when it is considered appropriate by the leadership disempowered those sectors of civil society that were advocating greater gender equality and could have played a key role in bringing about change. Cuba was not alone in struggling to find ways to advance gender equality.

The difficulty of changing cultural norms as opposed to instituting formal changes through government policies was amply demonstrated by events in Afghanistan and Iraq. Gender equality is allocated a prominent role in the restructuring of the political processes under way in Afghanistan and Iraq. Women activists in Afghanistan succeeded in getting important women's rights provisions included in the new constitution.[5] Afghanistan changed from a country where women's rights were severely restricted to a system that guaranteed gender equality under the law. In the area of political representation, the new constitution guarantees women's formal inclusion in political decision-making. Article 83 states that at least two female candidates from each province should be elected to Parliament. This constitutional provision was successfully implemented. In the September 2005 elections, 69 women, representing about 27 percent of the 249 members of the Wolesi Jirga, were elected. Similarly, Iraq's October 2005 constitution guaranteed women one-fourth of Parliament's 275 seats. Following the December 2005 electoral contest, women came to represent one-fourth of the National Council of Representatives. Yet women's participation in the Iraqi Parliament actually declined from the 31.5 percent reached in January 2005 to 25.5 percent in the December election of the same year. In the last elections, less than the required 25 percent of women candidates were elected. The Iraqi Electoral Commission required the political parties to replace elected male candidates with women that were lower on the list until the constitutional quota was fulfilled.[6]

Still, these improvements in the gender composition of the parliaments in both countries hardly reflected a change in societal consciousness toward greater substantive gender equality. Iraqi and Afghani women's rights activists argued that the female candidates, selected by male-dominated political parties that needed to fill established quotas, rarely represented women's interests. By most accounts, the new governments had only limited, if any, success in changing the predominant gender relations, which were strongly informed by traditional religious and cultural norms, and discriminated against women.

Thus, a sustained societal dialogue is key to moving toward substantive gender equality. In Cuba, an autonomous women's movement could play a central role in this process. A peaceful post-Castro transition requires a strengthening of civil society. Women have an important role to play in this coming transition, but they need to be given the institutional space to organize and develop an agenda independent from state and party influences. The Cuban leadership would be well advised not to repress those forces that seek change when they work within the system.

Cuban authorities were wrong in painting all of civil society with a counter-revolutionary brush. Instead, they would be better served by distinguishing legitimate oppositional challenges from subversive, foreign-sponsored activity. Diversity of opinion was curtailed in Cuba, and members of dissident groups faced potential imprisonment. According to estimates of European Union diplomats, there were 230 political prisoners before the April 2003 convictions of the 75 dissidents. Thus, political freedom in Cuba was restricted, a situation that called for reform. At this point, the Cuban officials who defend the status quo are helped by the misguided policies of the U.S. government. Ironically, the actions of the Bush administration have tended to undermine the credibility of the same societal forces it claims to advance. Particularly in the area of human rights, the United States lacked the moral authority to criticize Cuba while the Bush administration was running prison camps in Guantánamo and elsewhere, in open defiance of internationally accepted human rights standards.

An examination of the Cuban election process brought to the forefront the problems inherent in a one-party state. Although the party was not formally involved in the election process, it clearly shaped and influenced the selection of candidates through mass organizations and the candidacy commissions. The problems of the Cuban model, however, went beyond the Communist party's hegemony and concerned the party's internal democracy. A party insider, alluding to the lack of internal democracy, put it succinctly: "The problem is not the party. The problem is the style of democracy within the party."[7] María López Vigil, a student of the Cuban revolution who views the system with supportive eyes, argued recently that "only a revamping of the cultural and political attitudes of paternalism, verticalism, bureaucratism, and authoritarianism can allow Cuba to successfully address the tremendous challenges it faces at the turn of this century."[8]

The Women's Federation played a role that mirrored problems observed in the case of the Communist party. The FMC successfully stifled the emergence of an independent women's movement that could challenge its authority. The deactivation of Magín (the Association of Women Communication Workers) was a case in point. The federation prevented the existence of alternative independent voices articulating women's interests and by so doing locked itself into a time warp. FMC officials felt increasingly under attack, to the point that they were no longer capable of accepting any kind of criticism, even constructive criticism. The official FMC position held that the Cuban revolution's achievements in the area of women's rights were without parallel, at least in the region. Thus, there was no need to reflect on whether progress was being made toward substantive gender equality.

Ricardo Alarcón emphasized that two key reasons explained why women did not make greater strides in increasing their representation in positions of power: "[The] special period and the persistence of *machismo*. Because the special period brings with it material difficulties of every type, in the first place in the household, in the home. These difficulties fall primarily on women because of *machismo*. It would not have to be this way, but it is."[9] The "Special Period in Peacetime," declared by President Castro in mid-1990 as Communist regimes in Eastern Europe were dissolving, indeed brought economic hardships to all Cubans and particularly to women who had to focus much of their energy on coping with the ensuing economic crisis. Of even greater significance, however, was the lack of support from the party leadership for increasing the number of women in the top decision-making positions.

In this book I have sought to provide evidence for the thesis that gender equality policies pursued by revolutionary Marxist regimes, like that of Cuba, can lead to *unintended consequences;* namely, an exaggerated sense of the country's achievements regarding substantive gender equality. The successful implementation of social and economic policies benefiting women has effectively lulled the people and the Cuban leadership into the belief that traditional gender relations have been transformed in a more substantive way than the record supported. Although the achievements of revolutionary programs in support of gender equality were substantial, they were mostly restricted to the formal sphere. In the end, the in-depth analysis presented in this study demonstrates that Cuba had succeeded more at the level of formal gender equality than in a substantive transformation of society toward equal rights for women and men.

A 2002 evaluation of the government's actions in implementing the Beijing accords found that "the work group complained that after five years of having the National Plan of Action in force and following its first evaluation, no concrete advances can be determined in the majority of measures."[10] This lack of progress was attributed to the failure of the responsible organisms to coordinate their actions and to insufficient attention given to whether the measures were being implemented. Responsible officials at the national level did not ensure that the necessary measures were taken at the lower levels of government.[11]

The way relationships of power between women and men are constructed is very subtle. The real story frequently hides behind the indicators that show advances in formal gender equality. Even apparent improvements toward greater gender equality conceal, at times, continued discriminatory realities. Sonnia Moro has articulated this point eloquently:

> Gender inequities reconstitute themselves. For example, [the field of] medicine used to be in its majority masculine. Today there are more female than male doctors in Cuba, but the male doctors are in the cutting-edge fields, for example in transplants, and the female doctors are in pediatrics. . . . Take the field of surgery, for example: there are female surgeons. I don't want to say that they don't exist. However, if there are more female than male doctors, why are there so few female ones in the specialties with the greatest recognition? . . . A very subtle mechanism is operating here. . . . That is, once women break into a sphere there is a recomposition of gender inequities in the interior of this activity. To be a female doctor is not as prestigious as before. There are almost sixty thousand doctors in the country; it is no longer an elite.[12]

Cuban society was frayed and under stress as it entered a transition to the post-Fidel Castro period. Families have been torn apart by waves of emigration that had different roots: (1) Starting in 1959, people left Cuba out of opposition to the revolutionary government, resulting in a steady flow—sometimes a deluge, as in the Mariel exodus of 1980—of Cuban citizens moving to the United States; (2) Cubans who studied and worked in the former Soviet Union and its Eastern European allies at times chose to stay in their host countries; (3) This was also the case—although to a lesser extent—of Cuban military personnel who fought in Africa and Central America and for Cuban doctors and teachers sent on humanitarian missions around the globe; and (4) There is a new wave of mostly young Cuban women and some men who seek to escape the boredom and economic deprivations of their daily lives and marry citizens of Italy, Spain, Germany, and other European countries.[13]

Many Cubans are resentful of the impact the opening to tourism and the 1993 legalization of the dollar have had on their lives. Although Fidel Castro banned all dollar transactions in October 2004 in response to the strengthening of economic sanctions by the Bush administration, this reversal in policy had little impact on the economic reality confronted by Cuban citizens. Cubans without access to dollars or other foreign currencies have in effect become second-class citizens. The fact that many hotels and other tourist facilities are off-limits to ordinary Cubans leaves many citizens in a state of discontent, even though they understand the reasons for these restrictive measures. "Cubans cannot enter the Hotel Cohiba. I have been to the Hotel Cohiba. Cubans do enter into the lobby. You can eat in the restaurant, you can drink in the bar, but you can't get a room. This is a measure taken to avoid *jineterismo* [a Cuban form of prostitution]. . . . However, before the Special Period everybody in Cuba could go to all the hotels that we had, any five-, four-, three-, or two-star hotel. I went to Varadero [the best-known Cuban beach] every year under the CTC plan for workers. It was very cheap and I enjoyed what today [only] the tourists enjoy. . . . One experiences this up close, to have a dollar or not to have a dollar, [the poor buying power of] the salary. A retired person lives in a situation that can be very tough. And about this we continue to talk. We definitely live in a situation that is economically very difficult, very hard. It is very difficult for people that don't have dollars. One can be a brilliant person, or a party militant with thousands of merits, with a tremendous revolutionary history, and still, today, a person can't even buy a can of soda."[14]

In light of the serious economic and political challenges confronting Cuba in the early twenty-first century, it is interesting that I found little concern in an informal survey of Cuban friends and acquaintances regarding the possibility of an impending violent transformation of their system of government. The background of my sources ranged from government supporters to those sharing a critical view of the revolutionary regime. Most responses showed great faith in the system's ability to cope with change:[15]

> We are not concerned about the possibility of violence. The struggle for power will be difficult but not violent. The transition [from Castro] will be arranged among Cubans. Fidel is preparing for the time of change. His group of advisers consists of young people.

> The majority of the population supports socialism. We have a strong, organized party and prepared people. There is little danger of violent transformation. No one wants to go back to be dependent on the United States.

> In Cuba no one worries about this. The preoccupation [with violent transformation] exists only outside the country. We are also not afraid of possible U.S. aggression. Women and men view this alike.

> When Fidel dies, nothing is going to happen. There will be internal struggles within the system, but Fidel is not the system.

> People have memories of what happened at the Malecón in the early 1990s [police repressed a crowd of people expressing dissatisfaction with the economic and political conditions]. Something like this could happen when Fidel dies. But there is no real fear. No one is really worried.

I don't expect violent change. We have a way of life that is accepted. It cannot be changed that fast. Those of us over the age of fifty-five are committed to the revolution. As long as we are in power nothing will change.

Only occasionally did I encounter concern:

There is considerable worry regarding what is going to happen. There is a risk for violence. There is concern how the military is going to handle the transition.

Yes, there is fear of violent change when Fidel dies. There is fear that the exiles in Miami will want their properties back. We listen to the threats made on Radio Martí. My neighbor received a letter from Miami telling him to get ready to give his house back.

Admittedly, this survey has no validity from a scientific point of view, but it is indicative of how Cuban citizens who basically support the government view the question of regime change. Not surprisingly, statements by members of the Cuban exile community presented a different picture. In contrast with the opinion inside the country, there was the expectation that future changes in Cuba would be violent. For example, a former Cuban ambassador to the United Nations who recently defected argued that many aspects of Cuban life could produce a social explosion. In his view, "there is a lot of concern among the elite that this could occur."[16] If this was indeed the case, elite concerns did not manifest themselves in the voices of my small sample of Cuban citizens. Leaders of the Cuban exile community in Florida have predicted for years that Cuba will soon be engulfed in violence, only to be proven wrong by Fidel Castro's continuation in power.

Considering the difficult political and economic conditions, it is surprising that Cubans exhibited this degree of confidence. Cubans were not concerned about violent change, regardless of whether they were government officials, party militants, or regular citizens. One possible explanation why respondents maintained that any transition would be peaceful could be that people were simply afraid to speak their mind. There were obviously some people who were reluctant to share their true views in an interview, particularly if these views could be perceived as being critical of the government. In general, however, I do not believe "fear" to be a valid explanation. I have known several of my respondents for years and have built relationships of mutual trust. In the Cuban context it is not a "taboo issue" to talk about the possibility of violence.

An alternative hypothesis would be a "psychological" interpretation: people did not want to face this potential reality since any violent change would imply a drastic change in their living conditions. The revolution has profoundly altered the socioeconomic and political reality of the Cuban people. Therefore, any regime change would greatly affect the life of the average citizen. For example, most Cubans live in apartments and houses they have been allocated by government authorities for which they pay only a nominal rent. They would be greatly threatened were prior owners allowed to reclaim their properties or to charge market rent prices.

While one can speculate regarding the reasons, the fact remains that few people expressed concern about violent change. There were no apparent gender disparities—women and men appeared to think alike on these issues. Instead, differences existed between the generations. One source emphasized that people over fifty-five years old tended to be supportive of the system. The generation that grew up during the early years of the revolution, and those among the older generation that still remember the reality before the revolution, were in general strongly supportive of the government. As Katherine Gordy noted recently, the discontent this generation feels manifests itself not as opposition to the socialist system itself but as disappointment that the socialist principles—such as equality and solidarity—that this generation fought for are increasingly being abandoned.[17]

In contrast, young people were more likely to express discontent. A middle-aged supporter of the revolutionary process argued that a critical view from the younger generations was to be expected: "It is the generation of the fifteen- to thirty-five-year-olds that must be critical. They are the ones who must renovate the system. Fix the things that don't work."[18]

Whereas many young people were discontent with the government, others were energized on behalf of the regime during "the battle for Elián." At a time when the government was under severe strain due to the difficult economic situation, the Elián González case became the perfect rallying cry. Sonnia Moro noted the irony that the actions by the U.S. government had once again unified the country:

[They] were so brilliant as to create the Elián case to unite the people in an incredible way and to give a new generation the motivation to talk, to fight, to be patriotic. They gave the people a motivation. I have a twelve-year-old granddaughter. Well, my granddaughter who had not experienced any of this went to the marches. . . . What this case did was to create a new generation of kids and adolescents who have once again become motivated.[19]

Youth leaders sympathetic to the revolution shared this view. Ana Margarita Moreno, the FEM representative on the National Election Commission, emphasized: "The case of Elián brought a sense of renewal to our people. Starting with the abduction of Elián, began what is now called the 'Battle of Ideas.' The 'Battle of Ideas' started on behalf of the boy Elián. It was a genuine expression of the people who joined the leadership of the revolution, the leadership of the party [in the search] for the boy's rescue."[20]

Societal change takes time and is a complex process. New values must be transmitted to a new generation. In the area of gender equality, female leaders acknowledged some positive changes. Deputy Ana María Moreno argued that "the children [of female leaders] did not appreciate it that their mother was away from the home for a long time. Now they see that this is being recognized socially, and the children also start to change their thinking."[21] The question remained whether the Cuban leadership would be effective in communicating with a generation of young people that took the revolution's achievements for granted and resented the economic deprivation prevailing in the country. This would require an open, frank, public dialogue, an area in which Cuba was deficient.

Official Cuba, represented by the party and FMC leadership, was mostly in denial regarding women's limited participation in positions of power. At an individual level, however, most officials acknowledged that women's role in decision-making had to be strengthened. The problem with the official view, which emphasized Cuba's progress in guaranteeing women's social and economic rights and pointed to the high levels of women's formal political participation, was that it inhibited a public debate on how to transform prevailing gender relations. Until the party initiates such a dialogue, little will change.

Cuban exceptionalism is a problem here. Cuban officials feel the need to present a picture of harmony both for internal and external consumption. In Cuba, the struggle for gender equality is supposed to take place without societal discord. Concepción Campa affirmed this point of view:

> I know it [the struggle for gender equality] takes place in all countries, but here [it happens] without a fight. Because in other countries it happens with the women united in a corner fighting against the men. Here it is not like this. Here it is harmonious. Here it involves the search for equilibrium. [José] Martí said it: "No nation can be happy if it does not have equilibrium of the feminine and the masculine in equality of conditions."[22]

In their struggle to transform current realities, Cuba's female leaders need to build new alliances. Some female leaders are continuing in their efforts to build an independent women's movement that would complement the FMC. In other areas, however, alliance building is still in its beginning phases. Female leaders are increasingly aware that they need new strategies to defend their hard-won gains in the struggle for gender equality and to take the fight to new arenas. The most significant effort needs to be directed toward establishing the missing link—an alliance between the sexes.

The new millennium poses a central challenge for female leaders inside and outside the party establishment who are fighting for greater gender equality. They need to work on building a new alliance that includes men. In the end, only the joint efforts of both sexes can lead to a successful transformation of society based on democratic governance and gender equality. This is obviously a long-term process, but it must be initiated, regardless of the direction of Cuba's future.

A transition in Cuban politics is inevitable, as even the longevity of Fidel Castro's revolutionary leadership must come to its natural conclusion. Contrary to predictions by the Cuban exile community, Castro's death is not likely to lead to a cataclysm. The Cuban authorities had planned for a smooth transition, and daily government operations were already in the hands of a new generation of leaders.

The events of August 2006 confirmed this view. Fidel Castro surprised the world when he temporarily transferred power to his brother, Raúl, in order to undergo surgery for intestinal bleeding. In an August 2 message to "the people of Cuba and the friends in the world" the Cuban president acknowledged the seriousness of his health problems while declaring his health a state secret: "I cannot invent good news, because it would not be ethical and if the news were bad, the only one to take advantage from it would be the enemy. In Cuba's specific situation, due to the plans of the empire [the United States], my state of health becomes a state secret."[23]

Once again, Fidel Castro appeared to confound his enemies. Although in ill health, he was succeeding in ensuring an orderly transition. Behind heir apparent defense minister Raúl Castro, a supporting cast of key civilian figures was waiting in the shadows to help ensure the survival of the revolutionary order. According to "the received wisdom in Havana," Raúl would "share power with a civilian triumvirate" consisting of foreign minister Felipe Pérez Roque, National Assembly president Ricardo Alarcón, and Carlos Lage, the man in charge of Cuba's economy.[24] Most significant, the transfer of power was going to be "institutional" in nature. Raúl Castro had already made this clear in June 2006, when he emphasized that the Communist party "as an institution, which assembles the revolutionary vanguard" would be the only force capable of inheriting Fidel's mantle of leadership.[25] The vision of "institutional succession" was subsequently ratified in the July 2006 plenary session of the PCC's Central Committee.[26] Women will have an important role to play in this ongoing transition, and their absence or inclusion will speak to the nature of any emerging post–Fidel Castro system.

Appendix: List of Dissidents Sentenced in April 2003 by Province

Pinar del Río

Victor Rolando Arroyo Carmona	26 years
Eduardo Díaz Fleitas	21 years
Horacio Julio Piña Borrego	20 years
Fidel Suárez Cruz	20 years

Ciudad de la Habana

Osvaldo Alfonso Valdés	18 years
Jorge Olivera Castillo	18 years
Ricardo González Alfonso	20 years
Pedro Pablo Álvarez Ramos	25 years
Roberto de Miranda Hernández	20 years
Julio Cesar Gálvez Rodríguez	15 years
Efren Fernández Fernández	12 years
Edel José García Pérez	15 years
Omar Rodríguez Saludes	27 years
Marcelo Cano Rodríguez	18 years
Oscar Espinosa Chepe	20 years
Mañuel Vázquez Portal	18 years
Hector Maseda Gutiérrez	20 years
Adolfo Fernández Sáinz	15 years
Mijail Barzaga Lugo	15 years
Carmelo Díaz Fernández	15 years
Nelson Aguiar Ramírez	13 years
Nelson Molinet Espino	20 years
Antonio Díaz Sánchez	20 years
Regis Iglesias Ramírez	18 years
Arnoldo Ramos Lauzerique	18 years
Martha Beatriz Roque Cabello	20 years
Raúl Rivero Castañeda	20 years
Hector Palacios Ruíz	25 years
Marcelo López Bañobre	15 years

Oscar Elias Biscet González	25 years
Orlando Fundora Álvarez	18 years
Ángel Moya Acosta	20 years
Miguel Valdes Tamayo	15 years
Miguel Galván Gutiérrez	26 years
Alfredo Felipe Fuentes	26 years
Hector Raúl Valle Hernández	12 years
José Ubaldo Izquierdo Hernández	16 years
José Miguel Martínez Hernández	13 years

Matanzas

Guido Sigler Amaya	20 years
Ariel Sigler Amaya	25 years
Ivan Hernández Carrillo	25 years
Félix Navarro Rodríguez	25 years
Diosdado González Marrero	20 years

Villa Clara

Librado Ricardo Linares García	20 years
Margarito Broche Espinosa	25 years
Lester González Penton	20 years
Arturo Pérez de Alejo	20 years
Omar Pernet Hernández	25 years
Omar Moises Ruiz Hernández	18 years
Antonio A. Villarreal Acosta	15 years

Sancti Spíritus

Blas Giraldo Reyes Rodríguez	25 years

Ciego de Ávila

Pedro Argüelles Morán	20 years
Pablo Pacheco Ávila	20 years

Camagüey

Alejandro González Raga	14 years
Alfredo Manuel Pulido López	14 years
Mario Enrique Mayo Hernández	20 years
Normando Hernández González	25 years

Las Tunas

José Luis García Paneque	24 years
Jorge Luis García Tanquero	20 years
Alfredo Domínguez Batista	14 years
Luis Enrique Ferrer García	28 years
Reinaldo Labrada Peña	6 years

Holguín

Prospero Gainza Agüero	25 years

Granma

Julio Antonio Valdes Guevara	20 years

Santiago de Cuba

José Ramon Gabriel Castillo	20 years
Claro Sánchez Altarriba	15 years
Luís Milan Fernández	13 years
José Daniel Ferrer García	25 years
Jesús Mustafa Felipe	25 years
Alexis Rodríguez Fernández	15 years
Leonel Grave de Peralta A.	20 years
Ricardo Enrique Silva Gual	10 years

Guantánamo

Juan Carlos Herrera Acosta	20 years
Manuel Ubals González	20 years

Isla de Pinos

Fabio Prieto Llorente	20 years

Source: Comisión Cubana de Derechos Humanos y Reconciliación Nacional
Note: This is the document that Cuban authorities confiscated in May 2003. I obtained it again from another source.

Notes

Preface.

1. Interview with Ricardo Alarcón, Havana, March 20, 2003.

2. Shayne, *The Revolution Question*, 156.

3. Agüero and Stark, *Fault Lines of Democracy in Post-Transition Latin America*, V.

4. I have previously explored this argument in the book *After the Revolution: Gender and Democracy in El Salvador, Nicaragua and Guatemala*. Several passages in the manuscript are taken from *After the Revolution*.

5. Navarro and Bourque, "Fault Lines of Democratic Governance: A Gender Perspective," 175.

6. Ibid., 176.

7. Ibid., 182.

8. Araújo & García, "The experience and the impact of quotas in Latin America," 100.

9. Huntington, *The Third Wave*.

10. Waylen, *Gender in Third World Politics*, 118.

11. Recent examples include: Domínguez and Shifter (2003), Diamond et al. (1997), Domínguez and Lindenberg (1996), Domínguez and Lowenthal (1996), Tulchin (1995), Linz and Stepan (1996).

12. For a recent example see Nicholas Guilhot, *The Democracy Makers*.

13. Diamond, "Introduction: In search of Consolidation," XIV.

14. Domínguez and Lindenberg, *Democratic Transitions in Central America*, 2.

15. Interview with Iris Echenagusía, Havana, June 29, 2002.

16. Kvinna till Kvinna, *Engendering the Peace Process*, 14.

17. Carver, *Gender is not a Synonym for Women*, 120.

18. Parvikko, "Conceptions of Gender Equality: Similarity and Difference," 48.

19. Bengelsdorf, "On the problem of studying women in Cuba," 41.

20. Ibid.

21. Interview with Ricardo Alarcón, Havana, March 20, 2003.

22. See the appendix for the information contained in this document.

Chapter 1. Gender Roles in the Revolutionary War

1. Luciak, *After the Revolution*.

2. Stubbs, "Revolutionizing Women, Family, and Power," 190.

3. López Vigil, *Neither Heaven nor Hell*, 148.

4. Ibid.

5. Wickham-Crowley, *Guerrillas and Revolution in Latin America*, 21.

6. Guevara, *Guerrilla Warfare*, 132.

7. Interview with María Teresa Peña, Havana, July 1, 2002.

8. Luciak, *After the Revolution*, Chapter 1.

9. Kampwirth, *Women and Guerrilla Movements*, 127.

10. Smith and Padula, *Sex and Revolution*, 24; Shayne, *The Revolution Question*, 122; Anderson, *Che*, 234.

11. Díaz and González, "The Self-Emancipation of Women," 20.

12. Anderson, *Che*, 234–36.

13. Ibid., 276.

14. Smith and Padula, *Sex and Revolution*, 30.

15. Ibid., 27.

16. Ibid., 28–29.

17. Guevara, *Guerrilla Warfare*, 132.

18. Anderson, *Che*, 321.

19. Guevara, *Guerrilla Warfare*, 132.

20. Wickham-Crowley, *Guerrillas and Revolution in Latin America*, 21.

21. Díaz and González, "The Self-Emancipation of Women," 20.

22. Interview with Nieves Alemañy, Havana, March 21, 2003.

23. Smith and Padula, *Sex and Revolution*, 30.

24. Ibid., 31.

25. Ibid., 24.

26. Ibid., 25.

27. Guevara, *Guerrilla Warfare*, 132–33.

28. Smith and Padula, *Sex and Revolution*, 28.

29. Anderson, *Che*, 320–21.

30. Smith and Padula, *Sex and Revolution*, 28.

31. I am grateful to Lorraine Bayard de Volo for bringing the historical importance of these two women fighters to my attention.

32. Guevara, *Guerrilla Warfare*, 133.

33. Shayne, *The Revolution Question*, 20.

34. Ibid., 34, 133.

35. Interview with Mavis Álvarez, Havana, Nov. 13, 2002.

36. Interview with Sonia Moro, Havana, Nov. 13, 2002.

37. Ibid.

38. Kampwirth, *Women and Guerrilla Movements*, 128.

39. See Kampwirth (2002, 2004) and Shayne (2004) for similar arguments.

40. See Luciak, *After the Revolution*, chapter 1, for a discussion of the Central American revolutionary movements and their gender composition.

41. Anderson, *Che*, 356–59.

42. Ibid., 400–401.

Chapter 2. Changing Gender Relations: The Social and Economic Sphere after 1959

1. See the epigraph for a similar emphasis by Fidel Castro, speech delivered at the conclusion of the Fifth National Plenary of the FMC, Dec. 9, 1966, cited in Stone, *Women and the Cuban Revolution*, 48.

2. Interview with Nieves Alemañy, Havana, March 21, 2003.

3. Randall, *Gathering Rage,* 37.

4. Ibid., 16.

5. Harris, *Marxism, Socialism, and Democracy in Latin America,* 188.

6. Stubbs, "Cuba: Revolutionizing Women, Family, and Power," 192.

7. Ibid.

8. Ibid., 191.

9. Díaz and González, "The Self-Emancipation of Women," 20.

10. Stubbs, "Cuba: Revolutionizing Women, Family, and Power," 198.

11. Molyneux, "Mobilization Without Emancipation," 282–83.

12. Molyneux's distinction of practical versus strategic gender interests is not without controversy in feminist circles. I consider her categories helpful in understanding Cuban reality.

13. Molyneux, "Mobilization Without Emancipation," 284.

14. For a discussion of Sandinista policies toward women, see Luciak, *The Sandinista Legacy,* chapter 6.

15. Molyneux, *Women's Movements in International Perspective,* 79.

16. Bengelsdorf, "On the Problem of Studying Women in Cuba," 37.

17. Interview with Mavis Álvarez, Havana, Nov. 13, 2002.

18. Vilma Espín, cited in Stubbs, "Cuba: Revolutionizing Women, Family, and Power," 195.

19. Shayne, *The Revolution Question,* 156.

20. Interview with Mavis Álvarez, Havana, Nov. 13, 2002.

21. Stone, *Women and the Cuban Revolution,* 16.

22. Ibid.

23. Stubbs, "Cuba: Revolutionizing Women, Family, and Power," 200.

24. *Código de Familia,* 11.

25. Stubbs, "Cuba: Revolutionizing Women, Family, and Power," 201.

26. Interview with Mavis Álvarez, Havana, Nov. 13, 2002.

27. Ibid.

28. Shayne, *The Revolution Question,* 142.

29. Interview with Mavis Álvarez, Havana, Nov. 13, 2002.

30. Aguilar et al., *Movimiento de Mujeres en Centroamérica,* 47.

31. Fernandes, "Transnationalism and Feminist Activism in Cuba: The Case of Magín," 439.

32. Stubbs, "Cuba: Revolutionizing Women, Family, and Power," 194.

33. See the quote in López Vigil, *Neither Heaven nor Hell,* 169.

34. Interview with Sonia Moro, Havana, Feb. 15, 1998.

35. Kvinna till Kvinna, *Engendering the Peace Process,* 14.

36. See the discussion on Magín in this chapter.

37. Interview with a member of the Magín collective.

38. Interview with a confidential source.

39. Vilma Espín, cited in Stubbs, "Cuba: Revolutionizing Women, Family, and Power," 196.

40. Shayne, *The Revolution Question*, 151.

41. Interview with Concepción Campa, Havana, Nov. 19, 2003.

42. Interview with Nieves Alemañy, Havana, March 21, 2003.

43. Ibid.

44. Interview with Concepción Campa, Havana, Nov. 19, 2003.

45. Stubbs, "Cuba: Revolutionizing Women, Family, and Power," 197.

46. Smith and Padula, *Sex and Revolution*, 54.

47. Stubbs, "Cuba: Revolutionizing Women, Family, and Power," 198.

48. FMC, *La cubana: de Beijing al 2000,* cited in Echevarría, "Mujer, empleo y dirección en Cuba," 2.

49. Stubbs, "Cuba: Revolutionizing Women, Family, and Power," 197.

50. Molyneux, *Women's Movements in International Perspective*, 88.

51. Randall, *Gathering Rage*, 132.

52. Stubbs, "Cuba: Revolutionizing Women, Family, and Power," 194–95.

53. At the 2003 official exchange rate, 1 peso equaled 1 dollar. In the parallel market, however, one could get about 25 pesos for 1 dollar.

54. Interview with Nieves Alemañy, Havana, March 21, 2003.

55. Smith and Padula, *Sex and Revolution*, 55.

56. Interview with confidential sources.

57. Interview with a confidential source.

58. Interview with Iris Echenagusía, Havana, June 29, 2002.

59. Shayne, *The Revolution Question*, 145; López Vigil, *Neither Heaven nor Hell*, 173.

60. For excellent accounts of Magín's brief history, see Fernandes, "Transnationalism and Feminist Activism in Cuba: The Case of Magín," 431–52; and Shayne, *The Revolution Question*, 145–50.

61. López Vigil, *Neither Heaven nor Hell,* 176.

62. See Sujatha Fernandes's telephone interview with Norma Guillard in Fernandes, "Transnationalism and Feminist Activism in Cuba: The Case of Magín," 441.

63. Fernandes, "Transnationalism and Feminist Activism in Cuba: The Case of Magín," 442.

64. Conversations with OXFAM field directors Martha Thompson and Minor Sinclair, Havana, Feb. 14, 1998.

65. Shayne, *The Revolution Question*, 146.

66. Fernandes, "Transnationalism and Feminist Activism in Cuba: The Case of Magín," 442.

67. The view presented here was supported by Sonnia Moro, one of Magín's founding members. Interview with Sonnia Moro, Seville, Spain, July 19, 2006.

68. This account is based on interviews with several members of Magín who prefer to remain anonymous.

69. Interview with Nieves Alemañy, Havana, March 21, 2003.

70. Ibid.

71. This was the term reportedly used by Raúl Castro.

72. Interview with Nieves Alemañy, Havana, March 21, 2003.

73. Gunn, *Cuba's NGOs*, 4.

74. Interview with a confidential source.

75. Interview with Nieves Alemañy, Havana, March 21, 2003.

76. For example, see chapter 5 for the role mass organizations play in the electoral process.

77. Interview with Orlando Lugo, Havana, April 30, 2003.

78. Interview with Mavis Álvarez, Havana, Nov. 13, 2002.

79. Interview with Orlando Lugo, Havana, April 30, 2003.

80. Ibid.

81. Interview with Orlando Lugo, Havana, April 30, 2003.

82. Ibid.

83. Interview with Mavis Álvarez, Havana, Nov. 13, 2002.

84. Ibid.

85. Ibid.

86. López Vigil, *Neither Heaven nor Hell*, 156.

87. Echevarría, "Mujer, empleo y dirección en Cuba," 5.

88. Ibid., 8.

89. Ibid.

90. Shayne, *The Revolution Question*, 156.

91. Ibid.

92. Kampwirth, *Feminism and the Legacy of Revolution*, 66.

93. Interview with a confidential source.

94. Interview with a confidential source.

Chapter 3. The Cuban Political System: Competing Visions of Democracy

1. Stubbs, "Cuba: Revolutionizing Women, Family, and Power," 192.

2. López Vigil, *Neither Heaven nor Hell*, 37.

3. Interview with Jesús García, Havana, April 30, 2003.

4. "Opinión pública: ¿Qué piensa el pueblo de su poder?" and "La democracia cubana frente al espejo," *Bohemia*, July 6, 1990: 4–9 and 10–11. See Azicri, *Cuba Today and Tomorrow*, chapter 5, footnote 59.

5. See Machado Rodríguez, "Democracia política e ideología," cited in Azicri, *Cuba Today and Tomorrow*, 120.

6. Azicri, *Cuba Today and Tomorrow*, 120.

7. Interview with Jesús García, Havana, April 30, 2003.

8. Interview with Roberto Díaz, Havana, Nov. 13, 2002.

9. Interview with Eduardo Freire, Havana, Nov. 14, 2002.

10. This process is discussed in detail in chapters 4 and 5.

11. August, *Democracy in Cuba*, 303.

12. Calculated based on data presented in Azicri, *Cuba: Today and Tomorrow*, 308–15.

13. Interview with Marta Harnecker, Havana, April 29, 2003.

14. For an excellent introduction to the centrality of José Martí to the Cuban revolutionary process, see Kirk, *José Martí: Mentor of the Cuban Nation*.

15. See quote in Kirk, *José Martí*, 16.

16. Ibid., 48.

17. Azicri, *Cuba Today and Tomorrow*, 121-2.

18. Bengelsdorf, *The Problem of Democracy in Cuba*, 113.

19. Iraida Aguirrechu and José Quesada, *Poder Popular*, annex.

20. August, *Democracy in Cuba*, 262.

21. See chapter 4 for a discussion of the electoral system's gendered impact.

22. Interview with Ricardo Alarcón, Havana, March 20, 2003.

23. Ibid.

24. Roman, *People's Power*, 160.

25. Ibid., 155–209.

26. For an elaborate account of the 1997–98 election process, see August, 299–373.

27. Ibid.

28. Constitución de la República de Cuba, article 82.

29. Interview with Leonardo Martínez, Havana, Nov. 12, 2002.

30. Interview with Ana María Moreno, Havana, Nov. 11, 2002.

31. Interview with Leonardo Martínez, Havana, Nov. 12, 2002.

32. Interview with Ricardo Alarcón, Havana, March 20, 2003.

33. Constitución de la República de Cuba, article 69.

34. Interview with Jesús García, Havana, April 30, 2003.

35. Mayoral, "Constituye la asamblea nacional sus comisiones de trabajo," 8.

36. Interview with Ricardo Alarcón, Havana, March 20, 2003.

37. Ibid.

38. Ibid.

39. Interview with Jesús García, Havana, April 30, 2003.

40. Interview with Ricardo Alarcón, Havana, March 20, 2003.

41. Interview with Ana María Moreno, Havana, Nov. 11, 2002.

42. Interview with Roberto Díaz, Havana, Nov. 13, 2002.

43. See chapter 4.

44. Interview with Jesús Garcia, Havana, April 30, 2003.

45. Interview with Ana María Moreno, Havana, Nov. 11, 2002.

46. Interview with Leonardo Martínez, Havana, Nov. 12, 2002.

47. A union member quoted in López Vigil, *Neither Heaven nor Hell*, 18.

48. López Vigil, *Neither Heaven nor Hell*, 44.

49. Ibid.

50. Interview with Ricardo Alarcón, Havana, March 20, 2003.

51. Azicri, *Cuba Today and Tomorrow*, 118.

52. See table 5.2.

53. On Alarcón's ballot were two additional candidates: a woman who served as president of the municipal council and a man of mixed race who was an assembly delegate.

54. Interview with Ricardo Alarcón, Havana, March 20, 2003.

55. Ibid.

56. Interview with Roberto Díaz, Havana, Nov. 13, 2002.

57. Gunn, *Cuba's NGOs*, 1.

58. Ibid., 2.

59. Cited in Human Rights Watch, *Cuba's Repressive Machinery*, 60.

60. Gunn, *Cuba's NGOs*, 4–5.

61. Proyecto Varela, 1–9.

62. "Cuban Assembly Rejects a Reform Project" *New York Times*, Jan. 25, 2003.

63. Miguel Álvarez, quoted in "Cuban Assembly Rejects a Reform Project," *New York Times*, Jan. 25, 2003.

64. Interview with Eduardo Lara, Havana, Nov. 13, 2002.

65. Constitución de la República de Cuba, articles 88, 42.

66. Interview with Eduardo Lara, Havana, Nov. 13, 2002. See articles 88 and 137 of the Cuban constitution.

67. "Dissident Payá wieder in Kuba nach 50-tägiger Auslandsreise," *Der Standard*, Internet edition, http://derstandard.at/ (accessed Feb. 3, 2003).

68. Interview with a confidential source.

69. Interview with Roberto Díaz, Havana, Nov. 13, 2002.

70. Ibid.

71. Interview with Ana María Moreno, Havana, Nov. 11, 2002.

72. Interview with Iris Echenagusía, Havana, June 29, 2002.

73. Interview with Sonia Moro, Havana, July 3, 2002.

74. Interview with Ricardo Alarcón, Havana, March 20, 2003.

75. Statement by Oswaldo Payá, according to a source who witnessed his presentation to a Washington audience on Jan. 6, 2003.

76. Arrington, "Female Castro Supporters Break Up Protest," Associated Press, March 20, 2005.

77. Quoted in Pérez, "Conferencia de prensa sobre los mercenarios al servicio del imperio que fueron juzgados los días 3, 4, 5 y 7 de abril."

78. Interview with Orlando Lugo, Havana, April 30, 2003.

79. Ibid.

80. European Union, "Re-Evaluation of the EU Common Position on Cuba," http://www.eurunion.org/legislat/extrel/cuba/cuba2003.htm (accessed June 22, 2005).

81. According to one widespread belief, the mother of one of the hijackers went to the prison in an attempt to bring her son some supplies, only to be told that he had already been executed. Many Cubans were also upset because the people executed were only in their early twenties, an age that was considered to constitute an ameliorating circumstance.

82. Interview with a confidential source, Havana, May 2003

83. Azicri, *Cuba Today and Tomorrow*, 127.

84. For a recent example, see Nicolas Guilhot, *The Democracy Makers*.

85. For a recent example, see Human Rights Watch, *Cuba's Repressive Machinery*.

86. Interview with Leonardo Martínez, Havana, Nov. 12, 2002

87. "EU Lifts Cuba Diplomatic Freeze," http://news.bbc.co.uk/1/hi/world/americas/4223397stm (accessed Jan. 31, 2005).

88. Interview with Orlando Lugo, Havana, April 30, 2003.

89. Interview with Marta Harnecker, Havana, April 29, 2003.

90. López, *Democracy Delayed*, 160.

Chapter 4. Party and State: Gender Equality in Political Decision-making

1. Epigraph source: Fidel Castro, speech delivered at the conclusion of the FMC's Second Congress, Nov. 25–29, 1974, cited in Stone, *Women and the Cuban Revolution*, 71.

2. Stone, *Women and the Cuban Revolution*, 16.

3. Inter-Parliamentary Union (Feb. 2006).

4. Azicri, *Cuba Today and Tomorrow*, 124.

5. Álvarez et al., *Situación de la niñez, la adolescencia, la mujer y la familia en Cuba*, 224.

6. Ibid., 225.

7. Álvarez, "Poder sin quotas," 16.

8. Ibid., 17.

9. Interview with Leonardo Martínez, Havana, Nov. 12, 2002.

10. Duerst-Lahti, "The Bottleneck: Women Becoming Candidates," 15.

11. Interview with Eduardo Freire, Havana, Nov. 14, 2002.

12. Interview with Ricardo Alarcón, Havana, March 20, 2003.

13. Ibid.

14. Ibid.

15. López Vigil, *Neither Heaven or Hell*, 40.

16. Álvarez et al., *Situación de la niñez*, 223.

17. Interview with Jesús García, Havana, April 30, 2003.

18. Interview with Eduardo Freire, Havana, Nov. 14, 2002.

19. Htun, "Is Gender Like Ethnicity? The Political Representation of Identity Groups," 439.

20. Ibid.

21. Ibid., 450–51.

22. Interview with Roberto Díaz, Havana, Nov. 13, 2002.

23. Ibid.

24. Interview with Ricardo Alarcón, Havana, March 20, 2003.

25. Ibid.

26. Interview with María Josefa Ruíz, Havana, Nov. 11, 2002.

27. Ibid.

28. Interview with Mavis Álvarez, Havana, Nov. 13, 2002.

29. Interview with Nieves Alemañy, Havana, March 21, 2003.

30. Interview with Eduardo Freire, Havana, Nov. 14, 2002.

31. Interview with Roberto Díaz, Havana, Nov. 13, 2002.

32. Interview with Leonardo Martínez, Havana, Nov. 12, 2002.

33. Interview with Eduardo Freire, Havana, Nov. 14, 2002.

34. Inter-Parliamentary Union, *Women in Politics: 2005*.

35. Interview with Ricardo Alarcón, Havana, March 20, 2003.

36. Stubbs, "Cuba: Revolutionizing Women, Family, and Power," 196.

37. Rodríguez Calderón, "Queda mucho por andar," 29–30.

38. Azicri, *Cuba: Today and Tomorrow*, appendix E.

39. Bengelsdorf, "On the Problem of Studying Women in Cuba," 44.

40. Azicri, *Cuba: Today and Tomorrow*, 109.

41. Smith and Padula, *Sex and Revolution*, 182.

42. Azicri, *Cuba: Today and Tomorrow*, 318.

43. The Isle of Youth is commonly included as one of Cuba's provinces although it only has a municipal party committee.

44. A little anecdote here is very telling and helps one understand Cuban reality and the current state of gender relations: the Castro name has so much prestige in Cuba that Vilma Espín, arguably the preeminent female leader in Cuba, reverted her name back to Vilma Espín Castro, once she had divorced her second husband who had succeeded Raúl.

45. Randall, *Gathering Rage*, 152; Rodríguez Calderón, "Queda mucho por andar," 30.

46. *Granma*, Oct. 11, 1997.

47. Interview with María Josefa Ruíz, Havana, Nov. 11, 2002.

48. Anita Snow, "Communist Cuba's Military Marks 49 Years," http://www.iiss.org/whats-new/iiss-in-the-press/press-coverage-2005/december-2005/cubas-military-celebrates-49-years (accessed June 25, 2006).

49. I am indebted to Lorraine Bayard de Volo for bringing this point to my attention.

50. Interview with Concepción Campa, Havana, Nov. 19, 2003.

51. Ibid.

52. Interview with a confidential source.

53. Interview with Mavis Álvarez, Havana, Nov. 13, 2002.

54. Interview with Concepción Campa, Havana, Nov. 19, 2003.

55. Interview with Otto Rivero, Havana, March 19, 2003.

56. Ibid.

57. Ibid.

58. Interview with Nieves Alemañy, Havana, March 21, 2003.

59. This view is based on interviews with several female deputies.

60. Internal document.

61. II Seminario Nacional de Evaluación, *Plan de acción de seguimiento a la conferencia mundial sobre la mujer de Beijing*, 13.

Chapter 5. Gender Equality and Electoral Politics: The 2002–3 National Elections

1. Interview with Eduardo Freire, Havana, Nov. 14, 2002.

2. Interview with Roberto Díaz, Havana, Nov. 13, 2002.

3. In *Democracy in Cuba and the 1997–98 Elections*, August provides a rich, detailed account of the 1997–98 election process.

4. Interview with Eduardo Freire, Havana, Nov. 14, 2002.

5. Interview with Ana Margarita Morejón, Havana, Nov. 15, 2002.

6. Ibid.

7. August, *Democracy in Cuba and the 1997–98 Elections*, 302.

8. Interview with Leonardo Martínez, Havana, Nov. 12, 2002.

9. Álvarez, "Poder sin quotas," 4.

10. Interview with Eduardo Freire, Havana, Nov. 14, 2002.

11. Interview with Eduardo Lara, Havana, Nov. 13, 2002.

12. Interview with María Josefa Ruíz, Havana, Nov. 11, 2002.

13. Interview with Eduardo Lara, Havana, Nov. 13, 2002.

14. Roman, *People's Power*, 85.

15. Ibid., 83–84.

16. Interview with María Josefa Ruíz, Havana, Nov. 11, 2002.

17. Juan Marrero, "Más de 8 millones de cubanos a las urnas este domingo," *Granma Internacional*, Oct. 18, 2002 (Internet edition).

18. I had the privilege to be invited to the constituent assembly of the municipal council of Havana Vieja on March 22, 2003. On this occasion I observed the election process of the council's leadership.

19. Interview with Ana María Moreno, Havana, Nov. 11, 2002.

20. Marelys Valencia, "Primera fase de las elecciones generales," *Granma Internacional*, Oct. 22, 2002 (Internet edition).

21. Lourdes Pérez, "Tres circunscripciones este miércoles a tercera vuelta electoral," *Granma Internacional*, Oct. 29, 2002 (Internet edition).

22. "Kuba: Raúl toppt Fidel," *Der Standard*, http://derstandard.at/ (accessed Feb. 3, 2003).

23. Interview with Roberto Díaz, Havana, Nov. 13, 2002.

24. See chapter 3.

25. At this point, there are three female first secretaries.

26. See table 5.5.

27. For this point, I am indebted to Sonia Moro.

28. I am indebted to Peter Roman for this point.

Chapter 6. Conclusion: Gender Equality and Democratization

1. Epigraph source: Stubbs, "Cuba: Revolutionizing Women, Family, and Power," 203.

2. Dahlerup, *Women, Quotas and Politics*, 5.

3. Inter-Parliamentary Union, "The Participation of Women and Men in Decision-Making: The Parliamentary Dimension," 2.

4. Inter-Parliamentary Union (2005).

5. Mosadiq, "The New Afghan Constitution."

6. Luciak, "Conflict and a Gendered Parliamentary Response," 37–38.

7. Interview with a party insider.

8. López Vigil, *Neither Heaven nor Hell,* xviii.

9. Interview with Ricardo Alarcón, Havana, March 20, 2003.

10. II Seminario Nacional de Evaluación, *Plan de acción de seguimiento a la conferencia mundial sobre la mujer de Beijing,* 22.

11. Ibid.

12. Interview with Sonia Moro, Havana, Nov. 13, 2002.

13. I am indebted for this point to Sonia Moro.

14. Interview with Iris Echenagusía, Havana, June 29, 2002.

15. These quotes are based on interviews conducted during 2002–3.

16. Gedda, "Defector warns of 'Social Explosion' in Cuba," A09.

17. Presentation by Katherine Gordy, "Cuba Today" conference, Bildner Center, New York, Oct. 2004.

18. Interview with a confidential source, Havana, April 2003.

19. Interview with Sonia Moro, Havana, Nov. 13, 2002.

20. Interview with Ana Margarita Morejón, Havana, Nov. 15, 2002.

21. Interview with Ana María Moreno, Havana, Nov. 11, 2002.

22. Interview with Concepción Campa, Havana, Nov. 19, 2003.

23. Granma International, "Mensaje del comandante en jefe al pueblo de Cuba y a los amigos del mundo." http://www.granma.cu/español/2006/agosto/mier2/mensaje.html (accessed on August 2, 2006).

24. Anderson, "Castro's Last Battle: Can the revolution outlive its leader?" 47.

25. Raúl Castro quoted in Vicent, "¿Y después de Castro, qué?" 2.

26. Vicent, "¿Y después de Castro, qué?" 3.

Bibliography

Author Interviews

Abreu, Ramiro. Official of the Central Committee of the Cuban Communist party in charge of Central America. Havana, Feb. 13, 1998; July 20, 1999; Oct. 27, 1999; and Feb. 13, 2002.

Aguilar, Carolina. Member of the National Committee of the Cuban Women's Federation (FMC). Havana, Nov. 17, 2000.

Alarcón, Ricardo. President of the Cuban National Assembly. Havana, March 20, 2003.

Alemañy, Nieves. Member of the National Assembly and member of the National Committee of the Cuban Women's Federation (FMC). Havana, March 21, 2003.

Álvarez, Mavis. Director of International Relations, Cuban Small Farmers Movement (ANAP). Havana, July 21, 1999; Oct. 25, 1999; Nov. 11, 2000; July 3, 2002; Nov. 13, 2002; and April 30, 2003.

Álvarez, Mayda. Member of the National Committee of the Cuban Women's Federation (FMC). Havana, Nov. 21, 2003.

Álvarez, Miguel. Special Assistant to Ricardo Alarcón, president of Parliament. Havana, July 21, 1999.

Arce, Mercedes. Director of Ayuda Popular Noruega. Havana, July 21, 1999, and Nov. 13, 2000.

Arucha, Magalys. Director of International Relations of the FMC. Havana, Feb. 12, 2002.

Breteché, Olivier. Representative of the European Commission. Havana, Feb. 12, 2002.

Camilleri, Giovanni. Principal Advisor to the United Nations Development Program (UNDP) in Cuba. Havana, Nov. 15, 2002.

Campa, Concepción. Member of the Politburo of the Cuban Communist party and Member of the National Committee of the Cuban Women's Federation (FMC). Havana, Nov. 19, 2003.

Díaz Sotolongo, Roberto. Minister of Justice and president of the National Election Commission. Havana, Nov. 13, 2002.

Echenagusía, Iris. Former delegate to Poder Popular. Havana, June 29, 2002.

Florén, Fredrick. First Secretary of the Swedish Embassy. Havana, April 29, 2003.

Freire, Eduardo. President of the National Candidate Commission and secretary general of the Cuban Confederation of Workers (CTC) in Havana. Havana, Nov. 14, 2002.

Frühling, Michael. Swedish Ambassador. Havana, Feb. 15, 1998, and Oct. 26, 1999.

García Brigos, Jesús. Former member of the Municipal and Provincial Assembly of Havana and head of the Institute of Philosophy. Havana, April 30, 2003.

González, Ruben. Professor. Havana, July 4, 2002.

Guillard, Norma. Cofounder of the women's movement Magín. Havana, July 5, 2002.

Halkjaer, Eivor. Swedish Ambassador. Havana, Nov. 11, 2000; Feb. 11, 2002; July 2, 2002; Nov. 14, 2002; April 29, 2003; and Nov. 21, 2003.

Harnecker, Marta. Director of the Memoria Popular Latinoamericana research center (MEPLA). Havana, April 29, 2003.

Konrad, Helga. Austrian Ambassador. Havana, Nov. 15, 2002.

Lara, Eduardo. Principal Advisor to the National Assembly's Commission of Constitutional and Juridical Matters. Havana, Nov. 13, 2002.

Lugo Fonte, Orlando. Member of the Council of State and president of the Cuban Small Farmers Movement (ANAP). Havana, April 30, 2003.

Martínez, Leonardo. Member of the National Assembly and Secretary of the Commission for Productive Activities. Havana, Nov. 12, 2002.

Martínez, Nidia Diana. Member of the Council of State, Havana, March 18, 2003.

Martins de Almeida, Luciano. Brazilian Ambassador. Havana, July 4, 2002.

Menzione, Elio. Italian Ambassador. Havana, Nov. 15, 2002.

Miranda, Elsa. Housewife. Havana, July 5, 2002.

Montero, Susana. Chair of Género y Escritura "Gertrudis Gomez de Avellanela," University of Havana. Havana, July 4, 2002.

Moreno, Ana Margarita. Member of the National Candidate Commission and official of the Federation of Middle School Students (FEM). Havana, Nov. 15, 2002.

Moreno, Ana María. Member of the National Assembly and secretary of the Commission of Health, Sports and Environment. Havana, Nov. 11, 2002.

Moro, Sonia. Cofounder of the women's movement Magín. Havana, Feb. 15, 1998; Feb. 12, 2002; June 28, 2002; July 3, 2002; Nov. 10, 2002; March 16, 2003; April 27, 2003, and Sevilla, Spain, July 19, 2006.

Newman, Lucia. Head of CNN office in Cuba. Havana, May 1, 2003.

Pavani, Raffaela. Italian diplomat. Havana, Nov. 15, 2002.

Peña, María Teresa. Cofounder of the Cuban women's movement (FMC), excombatant, and militant of the Cuban Communist party (PCC). Havana, July 1, 2002.

Proveyer, Clotilde. Head of sociology department, University of Havana. Havana, Nov. 13, 2000.

Ramírez, Consuelo. Writer. Havana, July 2, 2002.

Regalado, Roberto. Head of the Analysis Section of the Central Committee of the Cuban Communist party. Havana, Feb. 13, 1998.

Rivero, Otto. Member of the Council of State and secretary general of the Union of Young Communists (UJC). Havana, March 19, 2003.

Ruíz, María Josefa. Member of the National Assembly and secretary of the Commission of Education, Culture, Science and Technology. Havana, Nov. 11, 2002.

Secondary Sources

Agüero, Felipe, and Jeffrey Stark, eds. *Fault Lines of Democracy in Post-Transition Latin America*. Miami: North-South Center Press, 1998.

Aguilar, Leticia, et al. *Movimiento de mujeres en Centroamérica*. Managua: La Corriente, 1997.

Aguirrechu, Iraida, and José Quesada. *Poder popular: República de Cuba*. Havana: Editora Política, 2001.

Álvarez, Mayda, et al. *Elatorías: Casas y cátedras de la mujer y la familia*. Havana: FMC/UNICEF, 1999.

———. *Mujer y poder en Cuba*. Havana: FMC/UNICEF, 1999.

———. "Poder sin quotas: Mujer y acceso a la toma de decisiones en Cuba." Paper prepared for presentation at the 25th Congress of the Latin American Studies Association, Las Vegas, Nevada, Oct. 7–9, 2004.

———. *Situación de la niñez, la adolescencia, la mujer y la familia en Cuba*. Havana: FMC/UNICEF, 2000.

Anderson, Jon Lee. "Castro's Last Battle: Can the Revolution Outlive Its Leader?" *The New Yorker*. (July 31, 2006): 44–55.

———. *Che Guevara: A Revolutionary Life*. New York: Grove, 1997.

Araújo, Clara, and Ana Isabel García. "The Experience and the Impact of Quotas in Latin America." In *Women, Quotas, and Politics*. Ed. Drude Dahlerup. New York: Routledge, 2006.

Asamblea Nacional de Poder Popular. *Poder popular: República de Cuba*. Havana: Editora Política, 2001.

August, Arnold. *Democracy in Cuba and the 1997–98 Elections*. Havana: Instituto Cubano del Libro, 1999.

Azicri, Max. *Cuba: Politics, Economics and Society*. New York: Pinter, 1988.

———. *Cuba Today and Tomorrow: Reinventing Socialism*. Gainesville: University Press of Florida, 2000.

Azicri, Max, and Elsie Deal, eds. *Cuban Socialism in a New Century*. Gainesville: University Press of Florida, 2004.

Bengelsdorf, Carollee. "On the Problem of Studying Women in Cuba." *Race and Class* 28, no.2 (1985): 35–50.

———. *The Problem of Democracy in Cuba: Between Vision and Reality*. New York: Oxford University Press, 1994.

Blasier, Cole, and Carmelo Mesa-Lago, eds. *Cuba in the World*. Pittsburgh: University of Pittsburgh Press, 1979.

Brenner, Philip. *From Confrontation to Negotiation: U.S. Relations with Cuba*. Boulder, Colo.: Westview, 1988.

Brundenius, Claes. *Economic Growth, Basic Needs and Income Distribution in Revolutionary Cuba*. Lund, Sweden: Research Policy Institute, 1981.

———. *Revolutionary Cuba: The Challenge of Economic Growth with Equity*. Boulder, Colo.: Westview, 1984.

Cantor, Jay. *The Death of Che Guevara*. New York: Vintage, 1983.

Carver, Terrell. *Gender Is Not a Synonym for Women*. Boulder, Colo.: Lynne Rienner, 1996.

Castañeda, Jorge G. *Compañero: The Life and Death of Che Guevara*. New York: Alfred A. Knopf, 1997.

Castillo, Daisy Rubiera. *Reyita: Testimonio de una cubana nonagenaria*. Havana: Ediciones Verde Olivo, 2000.

Constitución de la República de Cuba. Havana: Editorial de Ciencias Sociales, 2001.

Deere, Carmen Diana, and Magdalena León. *Empowering Women: Land and Property Rights in Latin America*. Pittsburgh: University of Pittsburgh Press, 2001.

——, eds. *Rural Women and State Policy: Feminist Perspectives on Latin American Agricultural Development*. Boulder, Colo.: Westview, 1987.

Del Aguila, Juan M. *Cuba: Dilemmas of a Revolution*. Boulder, Colo.: Westview, 1988.

Diamond, Larry. *Developing Democracy: Beyond Consolidation*. Baltimore: Johns Hopkins University Press, 1999.

Diamond, Larry, et al. *Consolidating the Third Wave Democracies*. Baltimore: Johns Hopkins University Press, 1997.

Díaz Vallina, Elvira, and Julio César González Pagés. "The Self-Emancipation of Women." In *Cuban Transitions at the Millennium*. Ed. Eloise Linger and John Cotman. Largo, Md.: International Development Options, 2000. 15–31.

Domínguez, Jorge I., and Marc Lindenberg, eds. *Democratic Transitions in Central America*. Gainesville: University Press of Florida, 1996.

Domínguez, Jorge I., and Abraham F. Lowenthal, eds. *Constructing Democratic Governance: Mexico, Central America, and the Caribbean in the 1990s*. Baltimore: Johns Hopkins University Press, 1996.

——. *Constructing Democratic Governance in Latin America*. Baltimore: Johns Hopkins University Press, 2003.

Domínguez, Magalys Arocha. *Violencia contra la mujer*. Havana: FMC/UNICEF, 1999.

Duerst-Lahti, Georgia. "The Bottleneck: Women Becoming Candidates." In *Women and Elective Office: Past, Present, Future*. Ed. Sue Thomas and Clyde Wilcox. New York: Oxford University Press, 1998.

Echevarría León, Dayma. "Mujer, empleo y dirección en Cuba: Algo más que estadísticas." Havana, 2004 (mimeographed).

Eckstein, Susan Eva. *Back from the Future: Cuba under Castro*. Princeton, N.J.: Princeton University Press, 1994.

Federación de Mujeres Cubanas. *Así fue nuestro VII Congreso*. Havana: Editorial de la Mujer, 2000.

——. *La Cubana: de Beijing al 2000*. Havana: Editorial de la Mujer, 1996.

——. *Memoria: II Congreso Nacional de la Federación de Mujeres Cubanas*. Havana: Editorial Orbe, 1975.

——. *Memorias: VI Congreso de la FMC*. Havana: Federación de Mujeres Cubanas, 1995.

——. *Memorias del IV Congreso de la Federación de Mujeres Cubanas*. Havana: Editora Política, 1987.

Fernandes, Sujatha. "Transnationalism and Feminist Activism in Cuba." *Politics and Gender* 1, no.3 (2005): 431–52.

Fuente, Alejandro de la. *A Nation for All: Race, Inequality, and Politics in Twentieth-Century Cuba*. Chapel Hill: University of North Carolina Press, 2001.

García Brigos, Jesús P. *Gobernabilidad y democracia: Los órganos del poder popular en Cuba*. Havana: Editorial de Ciencias Sociales, 1998.

García Luis, Julio, ed. *Cuban Revolution Reader: A Documentary History*. New York: Ocean Press, 2001.

Gedda, George. "Defector Warns of 'Social Explosion' in Cuba." *Washington Post*, Aug. 13, 2002, page A09.

Gómez, Enrique Ubieta, ed. *Vivir y pensar en Cuba*. Havana: Centro de Estudios Martianos, 2002.

Gómez, Mayra. *Human Rights in Cuba, El Salvador and Nicaragua: A Sociological Perspective on Human Rights Abuse*. New York: Routledge, 2003.

Guevara, Che. *Guerrilla Warfare*. Intro. Brian Loveman and Thomas M. Davies Jr. Wilmington: Scholarly Resources, 1985.

Guilhot, Nicolas. *The Democracy Makers: Human Rights and International Order*. Irvington, N.Y.: Columbia University Press, 2005.

Gunn Clissold, Gillian. "Cuba's NGOs: Government Puppets or Seeds of Civil Society." *Cuba Briefing Paper Series*, no.7 (Feb. 1995), Center for Latin American Studies, Georgetown University.

———. "Cuba Today." Center for National Policy, Washington, D.C. April 2002.

Harnecker, Marta. *Cuba: Dictadura o democracia?* Cerro del Agua, Mexico City: Siglo Veintiuno Editores, 1984.

Harris, Richard L., and Carlos Vilas, eds. *Nicaragua: A Revolution under Siege*. London: Zed, 1985.

Horowitz, Irving Louis, ed. *Cuban Communism*. New Brunswick, N.J.: Transaction, 1989.

Htun, Mala. "Is Gender Like Ethnicity? The Political Representation of Identity Groups." *Perspectives on Politics* 2, no. 3 (Sept. 2004): 439–58.

Human Rights Watch. *Cuba's Repressive Machinery: Human Rights Forty Years After the Revolution*. New York: Human Rights Watch, 1999.

Huntington, Samuel P. *The Third Wave: Democratization in the Late Twentieth Century*. Norman: University of Oklahoma Press, 1991.

Inter-Parliamentary Union (IPU). "The Participation of Women and Men in Decision-Making: The Parliamentary Dimension." Background paper for the Expert Group Meeting on "Equal participation of women and men in decision-making processes, with particular emphasis on political participation and leadership." Addis Ababa, Oct. 24–27, 2005.

———. *Women in Politics: 2005* [educational poster]. Geneva: IPU, 2005.

Jonas, Susanne, and Nancy Stein, eds. *Democracy in Latin America: Visions and Realities*. New York and Westport, Conn.: Bergin and Garvey, 1990.

Jordan, Mary. "Castro Takes a Page from Foes' Playbook." *Washington Post*, July 25, 2002, page A15.

Kampwirth, Karen. *Feminism and the Legacy of Revolution: Nicaragua, El Salvador, Chiapas*. Athens: Ohio University Press, 2004.

———. *Women and Guerrilla Movements: Nicaragua, El Salvador, Chiapas, Cuba*. University Park: Pennsylvania State University Press, 2002.

Kruks, Sonia, Rayna Rapp, and Marilyn B. Young, eds. *Promissory Notes: Women in the Transition to Socialism*. New York: Monthly Review Press, 1989.

Kvinna till Kvinna. *Engendering the Peace Process: A Gender Approach to Dayton—and Beyond.* Stockholm: Kvinna till Kvinna Foundation, 2000.

Lavan, George, ed. *Che Guevara Speaks: Selected Speeches and Writings.* New York: Pathfinder Press, 1967.

Linger, Eloise, and John Cotman, eds. *Cuban Transitions at the Millennium.* Largo, Md.: International Development Options, 2000.

Linz, Juan J., and Alfred Stepan. *Problems of Democratic Transition and Consolidation.* Baltimore: Johns Hopkins University Press, 1996.

López, Juan J. *Democracy Delayed: The Case of Castro's Cuba.* Baltimore: Johns Hopkins University Press, 2002.

López Vigil, Maria. *Cuba: Neither Heaven nor Hell.* Washington, D.C.: Ecumenical Program on Central America and the Caribbean, 1999.

Lowenthal, Abraham F., and Jorge I. Domínguez. "Constructing Democratic Governance." Introduction to *Constructing Democratic Governance: Mexico, Central America and the Caribbean in the 1990s.* Ed. Jorge I. Domínguez and Abraham F. Lowenthal. Baltimore: Johns Hopkins University Press, 1996.

Luciak, Ilja A. *After the Revolution: Gender and Democracy in El Salvador, Nicaragua and Guatemala.* Baltimore: Johns Hopkins University Press, 2001.

———. "Conflict and a Gendered Parliamentary Response." Consultant report prepared for the United Nations Development Program (UNDP). Project on "Strengthening the Role of Parliaments in Crisis Prevention and Recovery," April 2006.

———. "Gender Equality and Democratization in Cuba," Report prepared under contract (CA/B7-6110/2000/02) for the European Commission, Oct. 2003.

———. *The Sandinista Legacy: Lessons from a Political Economy in Transition.* Gainesville: University Press of Florida, 1995.

Luxemburg, Rosa. *The Russian Revolution and Leninism or Marxism?* Ann Arbor: University of Michigan Press, 1982.

Machado Rodríguez, Darío L. "Democracia política e ideología: Una opinión después del V congreso del partido." *Cuba Socialista* 9 (1998).

Martí, José. *Latin American Integration.* Havana: Instituto Cubano del Libro, 1998.

Mayoral, María Julia. "Constituye la asamblea nacional sus comisiones de trabajo." *Granma,* March 18, 2003, page 8.

Molyneux, Maxine. "Mobilization Without Emancipation? Women's Interests, State and Revolution." In *Transition and Development: Problems of Third World Socialism.* Ed. Richard R. Fagen et al. New York: Monthly Review Press, 1986.

———. *Women's Movements in International Perspective: Latin America and Beyond.* London: Institute of Latin American Studies, 2001.

Mosadiq, Horia. "The New Afghan Constitution: How Women Succeeded in Ensuring Certain Rights and What Challenges Remain." *Critical Half* 1, no.3 (Summer 2005): 29–33.

Moses, Catherine. *Real Life in Castro's Cuba.* Wilmington: Scholarly Resources, 2000.

Navarro, Marysa, and Susan C. Bourque. "Fault Lines of Democratic Governance: A Gender Perspective." In *Fault Lines of Democracy in Post-Transition Latin America.* Ed. Felipe Agüero and Jeffrey Stark. Miami: North-South Center Press, 1998.

Oficina Nacional de Estadísticas. *La ocupación civil en Cuba*. Havana: ONE, 1999.

———. *Panorama económico y social de Cuba 2002*. Havana: ONE, 2003.

Omar, Manal. "In the Sea of Nation-Building: Anchoring Women's Rights in the Iraqi Constitution." *Critical Half* 1, no.3 (Summer 2005): 46–50.

Parvikko, Tuija. "Conceptions of Gender Equality: Similarity and Difference." In *Equality Politics and Gender*. Ed. Elizabeth Meehan and Selma Sevenhuijsen. London: Sage, 1991.

Pérez-López, Jorge F., ed. *Cuba at a Crossroads: Politics and Economics after the Fourth Party Congress*. Gainesville: University Press of Florida, 1994.

Pérez Roque, Felipe. "Conferencia de prensa sobre los mercenarios al servicio del imperio que fueron juzgados los días 3, 4, 5 y 7 de abril." Havana, April 9, 2003, mimeograph.

Pérez-Stable, Marifeli. *The Cuban Revolution: Origins, Course, and Legacy*. New York: Oxford University Press, 1999.

Proyecto Varela. Petition written by Oswaldo José Payá. Havana, March 6, 2001, photocopy.

Purcell, Susan Kaufman, and David Rothkopf, eds. *Cuba: The Contours of Change*. Boulder, Colo.: Lynne Rienner, 2000.

Ramonet, Ignacio. *Propagandas silenciosas: Masas, televisión, cine*. Havana: Instituto Cubano del Libro, 2001.

Randall, Margaret. *Gathering Rage: The Failure of Twentieth Century Revolutions to Develop a Feminist Agenda*. New York: Monthly Review Press, 1992.

Reed, Gail. *Island in the Storm: The Cuban Communist Party's Fourth Congress* New York: Ocean Press, 1992.

Rehn, Elisabeth, and Ellen Johnson Sirleaf. *Women, War, Peace: The Independent Experts' Assessment on the Impact of Armed Conflict on Women and Women's Role in Peacebuilding*. New York: United Nations Development Fund for Women, 2002.

Ripley, C. Peter. *Conversations with Cuba*. Athens: University of Georgia Press, 2001.

Robaina, Tomás Fernández. *Historias de Mujeres Públicas*. Havana: Instituto Cubano del Libro, 1998.

Rodríguez Calderón, Mirta. "Queda mucho por andar." United Nations–Cuba office, n.d. (unpublished report).

Roman, Peter. *People's Power: Cuba's Experiment with Representative Government*. Boulder, Colo.: Westview, 1999.

Rosendahl, Mona. *Inside the Revolution: Everyday Life in Socialist Cuba*. Ithaca, N.Y.: Cornell University Press, 1997.

Sánchez, Susana Montero, and Zaida Capote Cruz, eds. *Con el Lente Oblicuo: Aproximaciones cubanas a los estudios de género*. Havana: Editorial de la Mujer, 1999.

Sección Científica Militar, FAR. *Código de Familia*. Havana: Imprenta Central de las FAR, 1987.

II Seminario Nacional de Evaluación. *Plan de acción de seguimiento a la conferencia mundial sobre la mujer de Beijing*. Havana: Editorial de la Mujer. 2002.

Sengupta, Somini. "Voting May Be Life-and-Death Choice for Afghans." *New York Times*, http://www.nytimes.com, accessed Sept. 16, 2005.

Shayne, Julie D. *The Revolution Question: Feminisms in El Salvador, Chile, and Cuba.* New Brunswick, N.J.: Rutgers University Press, 2004.

Smith, Lois M., and Alfred Padula. *Sex and Revolution: Women in Socialist Cuba.* New York: Oxford University Press, 1996.

Stone, Elizabeth, ed. *Women and the Cuban Revolution: Speeches and Documents by Fidel Castro, Vilma Espín and Others.* New York: Pathfinder Press, 1981.

Stubbs, Jean. "Revolutionizing Women, Family, and Power." In *Women and Politics Worldwide.* Ed. Barbara J. Nelson and Najma Chowdhury. New Haven: Yale University Press, 1994. 190–207.

Suchlicki, Jaime. *Cuba: From Columbus to Castro.* Washington, D.C.: Pergamon-Brassey's, 1986.

Taber, Michael. *Fidel Castro Speeches: Cuba's Internationalist Foreign Policy, 1975–80.* New York: Pathfinder Press, 1981.

Tétreault, Mary Ann, ed. *Women and Revolution in Africa, Asia, and the New World.* Columbia: University of South Carolina Press, 1994.

Timossi, Jorge. *Los cuentos de Barbarroja.* Havana: Editorial de Ciencias Sociales, 1999.

Tulchin, Joseph S., ed. *The Consolidation of Democracy in Latin America.* Boulder, Colo.: Lynne Rienner, published with the Woodrow Wilson Center, 1995.

Unidad Revolucionaria Nacional Guatemalteca. "Personal Incorporado: Diagnóstico Socio-Económico." Guatemala City: URNG, 1997.

United Nations Development Program. *Human Development Report 2003.* New York: Oxford University Press, 2003.

United Nations Observer Mission in El Salvador. *Proceso de desmovilización del personal del FMLN.* San Salvador: Imprenta El Estudiante, n.d.

United Nations Research Institute for Social Development (UNRISD). *Gender Equality: Striving for Justice in an Unequal World.* Geneva: UNRISD, 2005.

Varela Project. http://www.puenteinfocubamiami.org/varela_project_003.htm

Vicent, Mauricio. "¿Y después de Castro, qué?" *El País.* (July 16, 2006): 1–5.

Waylen, Georgina. *Gender in Third World Politics.* Boulder, Colo.: Lynne Rienner, 1996.

Wickham-Crowley, Timothy P. *Guerrillas and Revolution in Latin America.* Princeton, N.J.: Princeton University Press, 1992.

Index

Page numbers in italics refer to figures and tables

Acosta Ferrales, Clodomira, 6
Affirmative action, 73–74, 84
Afghanistan, 60, 103; democracy and, xvii
Agricultural Cooperative (CAI), xi
Alarcón, Ricardo, xxvi, xxvii, 42–43, 45, 52, 54, 56, 69–70, 111, 122n53; on Cuban pluralism, 46, 48–49; on European Union relationship with Cuba, xiv; on foreign power in Cuba, 59–60; on gender quotas, 73; on opposition movement, 55; on unity vote, 49–50; on women in government, 79, 105
Alemañy, Nieves, 4–5, 13, 23, 74; on FMC, 27–28
Alliance building, 110–11
Álvarez, Mavis, 7, 16, 20; on ANAP, 32; on gender quotas, 74; INRA and, 29; on leadership in mass organizations, 84
Álvarez, Mayda, 65, 70–71
Álvarez, Miguel, 52
AMNLAE. *See* Association of Nicaraguan Women
ANAP. *See* Small Farmers Association
Anderson, Jon, 6
Argentina, 102; gender quotas in, xvi
Asociación de Agricultores Pequeños. *See* Small Farmers Association
Asociación de Mujeres Communicadoras. *See* Association of Women Communication Workers
Asociación de Mujeres Nicaragüenses, Luisa Amanda Espinoza. *See* Association of Nicaraguan Women
Association of Nicaraguan Women (AMNLAE), xi, 35
Association of Small Farmers. *See* Small Farmers Association
Association of the Independent Press of Cuba, 56

Association of Women Communication Workers (Magín), 25–28, 104
Associations Law, 52
Azicri, Max, 39, 41, 60

Baguer, Néstor, 56
Barbarroja. *See* Piñeiro, Manuel
Batista, Fulgencio, xix, 1, 3, 7, 13, 32
Battle of Ideas, 110
Bayard de Volo, Lorraine, 118n31, 125n49
Bay of Pigs, 62
Beijing Platform, 101, 105
Bengelsdorf, Carollee, xviii, 42, 79
Bourque, Susan, xvi
Brazil, 102
Bush, George W., 54–55, 104, 106

CAI. *See* Agricultural Cooperative
Campa, Concepción, 81, 84, 110; on feminism, 22–23; on Politburo member, 82–83
Candidate Commission. *See* National Candidate Commission
del Carmen Concepción, María, 81
Carter, Jimmy, 52–54. *See also* Varela project
Carver, Terrell, xviii
Cason, James, 55
Castro, Fidel, xiii, 3–5, 8, 13, 18, 24, 41, 61, 79, 82, 98, 105, 118n1; election of, 94; executions and, 58; female combatants supported by, 5; FMC supporting, 56; gender equality commitment of, 13, 23, 34, 63; gender quotas considerations, 74–75; prestige of name, 125n44; Celia Sánchez, relationship with, 4; transition afterward, 103–8, 111–12; as unity vote advocate, 49; Varela project and, 52; on women's emancipation, xv
Castro, Lidia, 5

Castro, Mirta, 5
Castro, Raúl, 4, 81, 82, 98, 111; election of, 94
Catholic Church, 2–3
CCS. *See* Credit and Service Cooperative
CDR. *See* Neighborhood Committees
CEA. *See* Center for the Study of America
CEDAW. *See* Convention on the Elimination
of All Forms of Discrimination against
Women
Center for the Study of America (CEA), xi, 51
Central America, xvi, xx, 102; gender equality
in, 16; gender and democracy of, 117n4;
revolutionary movements in, 9–11; women
organizing in, 20–21; women in revolution
of, 1
Central Committee, 79, 81, 86, 99
Central de Trabajadores de Cuba. *See* Cuban
Confederation of Workers
Centro de Estudios sobre América. *See* Center
for the Study of America
Chile, 102
Clandestine activities, 2
CNC. *See* National Candidate Commission
Código de Familia. *See* Family Code
Collazo, Odilia, 56
Comisión Cubana de Derechos Humanos y
Reconciliación Nacional, xxvii
Comisión Nacional de Candidatura. *See* National Candidate Commission
Comité de Defensa de la Revolución. *See*
Neighborhood Committees
Comité de Sufragio Feminino. *See* Women's
Suffrage Committee
Commission for Productive Activities, 44, 90
Commission of Constitutional and Juridical
Matters, 52–53
Committee of Scientific Women, 27
Committees in Defense of the Revolution. *See*
Neighborhood Committees
Communist Party of Cuba (PCC), xii, 24–25,
37, 40, 41, 48, *80*, 80–81, *81*; First Congress
of, 63; gender composition of, 79, 102, *102*;
Magín meeting with, 28; mass organizations
and, 29
Communist Youth Movement. *See* Union of
Communist Youth
Congreso Campesino. *See* Peasant Congress

Convention on the Elimination of All Forms of
Discrimination against Women (CEDAW),
xi, xviii
Cooperativa Agropecuaria. *See* Agricultural
Cooperative
Cooperativa de Crédito y Servicio. *See* Credit
and Service Cooperative
Council of State, 45–46, 57, 86; gender composition of, 78–79, 79; women on, 78–79
Credit and Service Cooperative (CCS), xi
CTC. *See* Cuban Confederation of Workers
Cuba: constitution of, 53; elections in,
xvii–xviii, xx; electoral politics and gender
equality, 88–99; foreign aggression in,
58–59; gender equality in decision making
in, xix–xx; government infiltrating opposition, 56–57; Helms-Burton law and, 58;
human rights of, xiv, 52, 56, 57, 104, 123n81;
Marxism of, 13–14; parliament of, xvi, xx;
patriotism of, 55; Plan of Action (2002), 87;
Revolutionary War of, 1–12; revolution contributed to by women, xix, 16–17; sensitivity
of, xiv; sexual division of labor, 79–80; U.S.
relationship with, xiii, 37, 58–59, 61–62, 104;
women's role in, xviii. *See also* Castro, Fidel;
Castro, Raúl; Communist Party of Cuba;
Cuban political system; National Assembly
Cuban Confederation of Workers (CTC), xi,
40, 87, 89, 90
Cuban Federation of Women. *See* Federation
of Cuban Women
Cuban guerrilla movements, 2–8
Cuban political system, 37–62; anomaly
of, 69–72; Associations Law, 52; Central
Committee, 79, 81, 86, 89; civil society,
51–60; elections, local and national, 93–96;
evolution and structure of, 38–51; labor and
maternity legislation, 15; local level, 64, 70;
mass organizations, 51–60; national level,
43–46, 63, 64, 70; nomination process,
89–92; pluralism, 46–49; Politburo, 79, 81,
86, 99; strengthening women's participation, 72–78; top party and state structures,
78–85; unity vote, 49–51; women in, 92, 100,
110. *See also* Municipal assemblies
Cuban Workers Central, *30*, 31
Cultural norms, changing, 36, 103

Democracy, xix; competing visions of, 37–62; Cuban versus Western, 46–47; exporting, xvii; formal, xvi, xviii; gender equality and, 100–12; substantive, xvi, xviii; women and, xv

Diamond, Larry, xvii

Díaz, Roberto, 40, 47, 51, 54, 73, 76, 88, 94

Discrimination, xi, xviii; positive, xx, 64, 72–74, 92

Dissidents, 56, 57, 104; list of sentenced, 113–15

Domínguez, Jorge, xvii

Duerst-Lahti, Georgia, 69

Echevarría, Dayma, 33–34, 34

Economic embargo, xiii–xiv

Education, xix, 15–17, 24, 31, 62

Elections, 38–39, 40, 65–67, 88–99, 93; in Cuba, xvii–xviii, xx

Emigration, from Cuba, 106

Engels, Friedrich, 14

Equality, xv. *See also* Gender equality

Espín, Vilma, 3, 4, 17, 81, 125n44; feminism of, 22

EU. *See* European Union

European Commission, xxvii

European Union (EU), xxvii, 39, 52, 57, 61, 102; as Cuba critic, xiii; human rights of Cuba and, xiv

Executions, 57, 58, 123n81

Family Code, 18–19

FAR. *See* Revolutionary Armed Forces

Farabundo Martí National Liberation Front (FMLN), xi, 102, 102; gender composition of combatants, 10, 10

Federación de Estudiantes de Enseñanza Media. *See* Federation of High-School Students

Federación de Estudiantes Universitarios. *See* Federation of University Students

Federación de Mujeres Cubanas. *See* Federation of Cuban Women

Federación Internacional Democrática de Mujeres. *See* International Democratic Federation of Women

Federación Nacional de Asociaciones Femeninas. *See* National Federation of Women's Associations

Federation of Cuban Women (FMC), xi, xix, xxvi, 2, 4–5, 13, 20, 31, 56, 76, 83, 89, 100, 104; creation of, 14–15; criticism of, 21, 25; early years of, 17–19; Family Code achievement, 18–19; gender quotas, Castro and, 74–75; Magín controlled by, 27–28; as NGO, 24–25; political participation of women, 23–24; Second Congress of, 63

Federation of High-School Students (FEEM), xi, 89

Federation of University Students (FEU), xi, 3

FEDIM. *See* International Democratic Federation of Women

FEEM. *See* Federation of High-School Students

Feminism, 17–18, 19, 35, 83–84; feminine versus, 22; FMC concern of, 23; gender and, 20–24

Fernandes, Sujatha, 26

Fernández de Cossio, Carlos, 58

Ferrer, Luis Enrique, 56

FEU. *See* Federation of University Students

Finlay Institute, 81

First Iberoamerican Women and Communication Congress, 26

FMC. *See* Federation of Cuban Women

FMLN. *See* Farabundo Martí National Liberation Front

Fourth World Conference on Women, 101

France, 102

Freedom, 52

Freire, Eduardo, 69, 71–72, 75, 78, 88; on CTC, 89

Frente Farabundo Martí para la Liberación Nacional. *See* Farabundo Martí National Liberation Front

Frente Sandinista de Liberación Nacional. *See* Sandinista National Liberation Front

FSLN. *See* Sandinista National Liberation Front

Fuerzas Armadas Revolucionarias. *See* Revolutionary Armed Forces

Gadea, Hilda, 11

García, Jesús, 45, 46, 48, 71

García, Yadira, 81

Gender bias, 92

Gendered revolutionary bridges, 7
Gender equality, 16, 105–6; Castro and, 13, 23,
    34, 63; consciousness raising for, 87; democ-
    ratization linked with, xv, 100–112; electoral
    politics and, 88–99; formal, xvi, xviii; in
    political decision making, 63–88; substan-
    tive, xvi, xviii; unintended consequences in
    politics, xv, xviii; unity vote and, 50
Gender quotas, xvi, 63–64, 72–78
Gender relations: Cuban Communist party
    and, 24–25; feminism and gender, 20–24;
    FMC creation, 14–15; health care and educa-
    tion for women, xix, 15–17, 44, 62; interna-
    tional influence, 20–21; mass organizations
    and women, 29–32; men, 21–22; strategic
    versus practical interests, 17–19; workforce,
    32–34
Gender roles: changing, 13–36; in Cuban revo-
    lutionary war, 1–12
Germany, 102, 106
Glass ceiling, of Cuban women, xx, 64, 82, 85
González, Elián, 70–71, 94, 109–10
González, Juan Miguel, 70, 94
Gordy, Katherine, 109
Grajales, Mariana, 4, 5
Grassroots organizations. See Mass organiza-
    tions
Guatemalan National Revolutionary Union
    (URNG), xii, 11; gender composition of
    combatants, 10, 10
Guerrilla Warfare (Guevara), 2
Guevara, Che, 2–7, 11
Guillard, Norma, 26
Gunn, Gillian, 51; on human rights, 52
Gutiérrez, Oniria, 3

Harnecker, Marta, 40, 61–62
Harris, Richard, 13
Havana Vieja, xxv
Health care, xix, 15–17, 24, 44, 62
Health, Sports, and Environment Commission
    of National Assembly, 44
Helms-Burton law, 58
Hernández, Melba, 3, 5
Hijacker executions, 57, 58
Housework/household responsibilities, 18, 65,
    70, 71, 80, 92, 105

Htun, Mala, 72
Human rights issues, xiv, 52, 56, 57, 104,
    123n81. See also Dissidents; Executions

INRA. See Institute of Agrarian Reform
Institute of Agrarian Reform (INRA), xii, 29
Instituto Nacional de Reforma Agraria. See
    Institute of Agrarian Reform
Integrated Revolutionary Organizations (ORI),
    xii, 40
International Democratic Federation of
    Women (FEDIM), xi, 20
Inter-Parliamentary Union (IPU), xii, 64
IPU. See Inter-Parliamentary Union
Iraq, 8, 60, 103; democracy and, xvii
Isle of Youth, 49, 81
Italy, 102, 106

Jineterismo, 106–7
John Paul II (pope), 53
Journalism Gender Circle, 27, 28
Juantorena, Alberto, 70

Kampwirth, Karen, 1, 2–3; on women as
    combatants, 8
Kirk, John, 41
Kirkpatrick, General, 59

Ladies in White, 56
Lage, Carlos, 111
Lara, Eduardo, 52, 90, 91
Latin America, 86; decision-making structures
    in, xvi; gender quotas in, xvi; women's vote
    in, 1
Leadership roles, 32–34, 34, 84
Lenin, 41
Lindenberg, Mark, xvii
Literacy campaign, 16, 17
López, Juan, 62
López Vigil, María, 49, 104
Lugo, Orlando, 29, 31, 57
Luxemburg, Rosa, 37

Machismo, 4, 70–71, 105
Machista culture, 31, 69, 71–72, 87
Magín. See Association of Women Communi-
    cation Workers

Mambisa (female independence fighters), 1
March, Aleida, 11
Mariel exodus, 106
Martí, Farabundo, 10, 60
Martí, José, 41, 83, 122n14
Martínez, Leonardo, 44–45, 61, 76, 90; on
   women in politics, 68
Marxism, 13–14, 40
Mass organizations, 29–32, 51–60, 84, 89–90,
   92
Men: decision-making power of, 33–34;
   gender equality and, 18, 21–22, 105–6; nomi-
   nating women, 65; political decisions of, 78;
   sexual equality of women and, 25; women
   resented by, 4
Mexico, xvi
Misión de Observadores de las Naciones
   Unidas en El Salvador. *See* United Nations
   Observer Mission in El Salvador
Molyneux, Maxine, 15
Montes, Segundo, xxviii
Morejón, Ana Margarita, 89
Moreno, Ana María, 44, 47, 48, 54, 92; on
   Elián González issue, 110
Moro, Sonnia, 7, 55, 120n67; on gender equal-
   ity, 106; on Elián González, issue, 109
Municipal assemblies, 42–43, 65–66, 66, 67,
   69–70, 90; election results, 93, 93–94; fe-
   male, 77; gender composition of, 96, 96–97

Naranjo, Arroyo, 92
National Assembly, xxvii, 43–46, 64, 86, 91,
   102; and Commission of Constitutional and
   Juridical Matters, 52–53; election results,
   93–94, 95; gender composition of, 68, 68,
   69–72, 97–98, 98; gender composition of
   candidates, 76–77, 77; Health, Sports, and
   Environment Commission of, 44; Standing
   Committee for Productive Activities, 68;
   time commitments of, 70; women's representation in, xx. *See also* Alarcón, Ricardo
National Association of Small Farmers. *See*
   Small Farmers Association
National Candidate Commission (CNC), xi,
   40, 43, 48, 50, 69, 75, 89–90; women and
   preferential treatment by, 76–78
National Council of Representatives, 103

National Election Commission, 40, 88
National Federation of Women's Associations,
   14
National Office of Statistics (ONE), xii
National Plan of Action, 105
National Revolutionary Movements, 3
National Union of Women, 14
National Women's Congress, 1
Navarro, Marysa, xvi
Neighborhood Committees (CDR), xi, 29, 30, 89
Netherlands, 101
NGO. *See* Nongovernmental organization
Nongovernmental organization (NGO), 24–25,
   51
Nordic countries, 101

OAS. *See* Organization of American States
Oficina Nacional de Estadísticas. *See* National
   Office of Statistics
ONE. *See* National Office of Statistics
ONUSAL. *See* United Nations Observer Mis-
   sion in El Salvador
OPP. *See* Organs of People's Power
Organizaciones Revolucionarias Integradas.
   See Integrated Revolutionary Organizations
Organization for Security and Cooperation in
   Europe (OSCE), xii
Organization of American States (OAS), 20
Órganos del Poder Popular. *See* Organs of
   People's Power
Organs of People's Power (OPP), xii, 41, 71, 86,
   91; gender composition of, 64–69, 96–98,
   99; women's participation in, 64–65, 65
ORI. *See* Integrated Revolutionary Organiza-
   tions
OSCE. *See* Organization for Security and
   Cooperation in Europe
OXFAM Canada, 26, 32

Panama, xvi
Partido Comunista de Cuba. *See* Communist
   Party of Cuba
Party for Human Rights of Cuba, 56
Payá, Oswaldo, 53, 56, 123n75
PCC. *See* Communist Party of Cuba
Peasant Congress, 29
Peña, Maria Teresa, 2

Pérez Roque, Felipe, 111
Pinar del Río, 96–97
Piñeiro, Manuel (Barbarroja/Red Beard),
    40–41
Pipeline theory, 69
Platform of Action, 101
Pluralism, 37, 46–49
Poder Popular. *See* Organs of People's Power
Politburo, 79, 81, 82–83, 86, 99
Positive discrimination, xx, 64, 72–74, 92
Powell, Colin, 53
Prostitution, 26, 106–7
Provincial assemblies, 67, 67–68; gender com-
    position, 97, 97
Puebla, Teté, 4

Quirot, Ana Fidelia, 70
Quotas. *See* Gender quotas

Randall, Margaret, 13; on FMC and PCC, 24
Red Beard. *See* Piñeiro, Manuel
Research, independent, xxv–xxvii
Revolutionary Armed Forces (FAR), xi
Revolutionary Directorate, 3
Revolutionary war (Cuba), 1–12
Revuelta, Natalia, 5
Rielo, Isabel, 4, 5
Rivero, Otto, 85
Rodríguez, Silvio, 70
Roman, Peter, 43, 91
Roque, Martha Beatriz, 56
Ruíz, María Josefa, 74, 91; on women in higher
    ranks, 81–82
Rwanda, 101

Sakharov Prize, 53
Sánchez, Celia, 3, 4
Sánchez, Elizardo, xxvii
Sandinista National Liberation Front (FSLN),
    xi, 9, 102, 102
Santamaría, Haydée, 3, 5
Scandinavian countries, 101
Shayne, Julie, xv, 1, 7, 22, 35; feminist mobiliza-
    tion, 17–18; on Magín, 26
Sida. *See* Swedish International Development
    Authority
Small Farmers Association (ANAP), xi, 7,
    16–17, 20, 29, 30, 30–32, 84, 87, 89, 90

Socialism, 13, 21, 107; Varela petition and, 54
Spain, 102, 106
Special Period in Peacetime, 105, 107
Standing Committee for Productive Activities,
    68
Stubbs, Jean, 100
Swedish International Development Authority
    (Sida), xii

Technology, 53–54
Terrorism, xiii, xxvi, 55
*Thesis: On the Full Exercise of Women's Equal-
    ity,* 63
Toricelli Law, 59
Track Two policy, of U.S.A., xxvi
2002–2003 election process, 88–99

UJC. *See* Union of Communist Youth
UNDP. *See* United Nations Development
    Program
UNEAC. *See* Union of Writers and Artists
UNICEF. *See* United Nation's Children's
    Fund
Unidad Revolucionaria Nacional Guatemalte-
    ca. *See* Guatemalan National Revolutionary
    Union
UNIFEM. *See* United Nations Fund for
    Women
Unión de Artistas y Escritores. *See* Union of
    Writers and Artists
Unión de Juventud Comunista. *See* Union of
    Communist Youth
Unión de Periodistas de Cuba. *See* Union of
    Cuban Journalists
Unión Nacional de Mujeres. *See* National
    Union of Women
Union of Communist Youth (UJC), xii, 85, 85
Union of Cuban Journalists (UPEC), xii, 28
Union of Writers and Artists (UNEAC), xii, 28
United Kingdom, 102
United Nations, xii, xviii
United Nation's Children's Fund (UNICEF),
    xii, 20, 26
United Nations Development Program
    (UNDP), xii, 26
United Nations Fund for Women (UNIFEM),
    xii, 26
United Nations General Assembly, xiv

United Nations Observer Mission in El Salvador (ONUSAL), xii, 10

United Nations Research Institute for Social Development (UNRISD), xii

United States (U.S.A.), xiv–xv, 63, 102; Cuba, relationship with, xiii, 37, 58–59, 61–62, 104; democracy in, 39, 48; dollar influence on Cuba, 106–7; economic embargo of, xiii–xiv; human rights of Cuba and, xiv; Interest Section, 55, 57; NGO's of Cuba and, 51; Track Two policy of, xxvi; World Trade Center attacks, xiii, xxvi. *See also* Bush, George W.; Carter, Jimmy

United States Agency for International Development (USAID), xii, xxvi

Unity vote, 49–51, 94

UNRISD. *See* United Nations Research Institute for Social Development

UPEC. *See* Union of Cuban Journalists

URNG. *See* Guatemalan National Revolutionary Union

USAID. *See* United States Agency for International Development

Varela project, 52–54, 56

Voting: unity vote, 49–51, 94; women's right to, 14–15. *See also* Elections

W. Averell Harriman Democracy Award, 53

Wickham-Crowley, Timothy, 2

Women, xi, xx, 1, 14, 20–21, 76–78, 101, 105–6; achievements in health and education, xix; affirmative action, 73–74; AMNLAE, xi, 35; as candidates, 65–66; CEDAW, xi, xviii; as combatants in Central America, 9–11; on Council of State, 78–79; of Cuban guerrilla movements, 2–8; Cuba revolution contributed to by, xix, 16–17; in Cuba's political system, 72–78, 92, 100, 110; decision-making power, xx, 86; democracy and, xv; emancipation of, xv; family role of, 23; farmers, 31; fears of working in politics, 83–85; FEDIM, xi, 20; as gendered revolutionary bridges, 7; gender relations and, 15–17, 29–32; glass ceiling of Cuban, xx, 64, 82, 85; in government, 79, 98–99, 105; Guevara on, 4, 6–7; increasing participation in politics, 72–78; invisibility of role, 4, 8; in leadership positions, 32–33, *33*; local level political presence of, xx, 98; Magín, 25–28, 104; mambisa, 1; mass organizations and, 29–32; men and, 4, 25, 65; in OPP, 64–65, *65*; oppression of, 15–16; privileging, 76; revolutionary movement contribution of, 1–12; revolutionary process affecting, xv; risks taken by, 6, 8; Sandinista policies toward, 119n14; scarcity of, in higher party ranks, 81–82; in top political positions, 78–85; Varela project and, 56; voting of, 14–15. *See also* Federation of Cuban Women; Gender equality

Women's Decade, 32

Women's Suffrage Committee, 14

Workforce, 32–34, *33*, *33*

World parliaments, gender composition of, *101*, 101–2

World Trade Center attacks, xiii, xxvi

Zapatero, José Luis, 61

Ilja Luciak, professor and chair of political science at Virginia Polytechnic Institute and State University, holds a J.D. from the University of Vienna and a Ph.D. in political science from the University of Iowa. He has written for Swedish, Austrian, British, Mexican, Nicaraguan, Salvadoran, and North American publications and has been a guest professor/fellow at Cornell University, Stockholm University, Innsbruck University, and the Central American University in Managua.

For the past twenty years the author has conducted field research in Latin America, focusing on gender equality and democratization. He has worked as a consultant for the United Nations Development Program (UNDP), the United Nations Development Fund for Women (UNIFEM), and the Swedish International Development Authority (Sida); has given numerous invited lectures; and has organized several international conferences on Central America and Cuba. He has been commissioned to contribute to the Ten-Year Evaluation of the Beijing Women's Conference, coordinated by the United Nations Research Institute for Social Development (UNRISD). In 2005–2006 Professor Luciak served as a consultant on gender and conflict for the UNDP project "Strengthening the Role of Parliaments in Crisis Prevention and Recovery."

Ilja Luciak completed a multiyear study, "Gender Equality and Democratization in Central America and Cuba," for the European Commission. His work resulted in two books, *After the Revolution: Gender and Democracy in El Salvador, Nicaragua and Guatemala* (2001) and the present volume, *Gender and Democracy in Cuba.*